Standards for ESL/EFL Teachers of Adults

Adult/Community

Workplace

College/University

Intensive English

English as a Foreign Language

 TESOL **Teachers of English to Speakers of Other Languages, Inc.**

Typeset in Berkeley Oldstyle with News Gothic Display
by Capitol Communication Systems, Inc., Crofton, Maryland USA
Printed by United Graphics Inc., Mattoon, Illinois USA

Teachers of English to Speakers of Other Languages, Inc.
700 South Washington Street, Suite 200
Alexandria, Virginia 22314 USA
Tel. 703-836-0774 • Fax 703-836-6447 • E-mail info@tesol.org • http://www.tesol.org/

Publishing Manager: Carol Edwards
Copy Editor: Lynne Lipkind
Additional Reader: Terrey Hatcher
Cover Design: Capitol Communication Systems, Inc.

ISBN 9781931185509
Library of Congress Control Number: 2008907787

Table of Contents

Acknowledgments

The realization of this book would not have been possible without the dedicated work of the following people.

Standards for Teachers of Adults Project Team:
> Robert B. Jenkins, Chair
> Maria E. Dantas-Whitney
> Mary Jeannot
> Jane E. Lockwood
> Patricia A. Porter
> Cynthia M. Schuemann
>> With contributions from Mary "Chris" Babowal

TESOL Task Force on Standards for Teachers of Adult Learners:
> MaryAnn Christison, Chair
> Donald Freeman
> Denise Murray
> David Nunan
> Sharon Seymour
>> Srisucha McCabe, staff liaison

TESOL Standards Committee:
> JoAnn Crandall, Chair 2006–2008
> Supreet Anand, Chair 2008–2010
> Candice Harper, Past Chair 2006–2007
> Mary "Chris" Babowal
> Tatiana Gordon
> Dorit Kaufman
> Silvia Laborde
> Paul Mahony
> Mary Lou McCloskey
> Faridah Pawan
> Beth Samuelson
> Anne Snow
> Richmond Stroupe
> Vilma Tafania
>> John Segota, staff liaison

TESOL members John Antonellis and Linda Tobash contributed to writing the performance indicators. UMBC doctoral student Rita Turner contributed to the glossary.

Thanks to all the reviewers and members of the TESOL field whose comments, feedback, and suggestions contributed to the development of these standards and this volume.

Special thanks to Jodi Crandall for her many contributions and efforts in the completion of this volume.

Preface

The *Standards for ESL/EFL Teachers of Adults* addresses the central issue, What does the profession of English language teaching consider to be effective teaching? This book is a culmination of years of study and discussion on the qualities and expertise necessary to be an effective teacher of English as a second or foreign language to adults. The standards have been developed to foster student success through effective teaching. Prospective teachers and seasoned veterans alike will find opportunities for professional development and self-reflection in the application of the standards. Teacher education programs and teacher trainers can give direction to their curricula by adopting the standards. The standards can also be used to establish hiring criteria for evaluating candidates and to assess teacher performance.

There has been a move toward performance-based assessment to measure a program's or a teacher's successes and failures. In response to this trend in education, teacher educators (e.g., Diez, 1998), researchers (e.g., Darling-Hammond, Diez, Moss, Pecheone, Pullin, Schafer, & Vickers, 1998), and teacher certification (e.g., INTASC[1], 2001) and accreditation agencies (e.g., NCATE[2]) have focused on outcomes of teacher education programs, rather than input (such as course content). This approach is characterized by

- describing the knowledge, skills, and dispositions needed for effective teaching

- having teachers demonstrate knowledge, skills, and dispositions

- assessing teacher performance of knowledge, skills, and dispositions by

  — linking assessment to performance

  — developing authentic assessment tasks

  — using multiple assessments

- recognizing the developmental nature of teaching

- acknowledging that teaching must have a positive effect on student learning

- recognizing that teaching and learning are context based

The global association Teachers of English to Speakers of Other Languages, Inc. (TESOL), has been engaged in developing standards for teachers of English as a second language (ESL) and English as a foreign language (EFL). The first set of standards was developed for P–12 teacher education in the United States. These standards have now been adopted by the NCATE, so that when teacher education programs in the United States apply for accreditation, they are required to address the TESOL standards if they have an ESL program at their institution. This book focuses on how applying the standards to develop the expertise of an instructor can foster learning by adult students in various ESL settings.

---

[1] Interstate New Teacher Assessment and Support Consortium
[2] National Council for Accreditation of Teacher Education

History

In 1999 the TESOL Board of Directors appointed a task force to develop a framework of standards for teachers who work with adult ESL learners in the United States. To initiate the project, the task force requested two white papers from the TESOL Teacher Education Interest Section to review research on teaching in formal and nonformal settings and the design of successful teacher education programs. A draft set of core standards and progress indicators was developed, and the task force collected feedback from various sectors of the field. The response from the field was that (1) such standards were needed in the profession, and (2) the draft standards were applicable in settings outside the United States as well. The draft standards were subsequently revised to be applicable in global settings.

The project was put in abeyance for a period of time. After the TESOL Standards Committee was created in 2002, the project was revived under the auspices of the committee. In 2004, the Standards Committee commissioned a team of writers versed in different settings for teaching English to adults. The team was to develop vignettes and other explicatory material for a complete volume. As the standards and progress indicators had already received considerable input and revision, the standards framework was approved by the TESOL Board of Directors in October 2006. *Standards for ESL/EFL Teachers of Adults* reflects the effort of these two groups, in consultation with the community of English language teachers, to use the standards for identifying the necessary qualifications of teachers of adult English learners in various settings: in the workplace, at the college level, in intensive English programs (IEPs), and in EFL programs.

Introduction

The mission of the global professional association TESOL is to ensure excellence in English language teaching to speakers of other languages. One of the methods TESOL has pursued to fulfill this mission is through the development of standards for English language teachers, learners, and programs. The current standards movement in the United States establishes the knowledge and skills that a teacher or student should possess (performance objectives) and states these objectives in the standards. The standards in this book, consistent with those of the National Board for Professional Teaching Standards (NBPTS), are performance based: They define what teacher candidates need to know and be able to do in order to teach effectively in particular settings.

Performance-based assessment differs from earlier teacher assessment designs, such as competency-based teacher education, because the standards set forth guidelines for effective teaching. Performance-based standards follow the logic that

- teachers can demonstrate the standards in their teaching

- teaching (teacher performance) can be assessed through what teachers do in their classrooms or virtual classrooms

- this performance can be detailed in "indicators," evidence that teachers can meet part of a standard

- the processes used to assess teachers need to draw on complex evidence of performance. In other words, indicators are more than simple how-to statements

- performance-based assessment is an integrated system rather than a checklist or a series of discrete assessments

- each assessment within a system has performance criteria against which the performance can be measured

- performance criteria identify to what extent the teacher meets the standard

- student learning is at the heart of teachers' performance

This approach clearly defines what TESOL considers effective teaching.

The standards for ESL/EFL teachers of adults are presented visually in Figure 1. At the center of the model is a circle, representing student learning. Learning is the central concern for all teachers and therefore occupies the center of the performance-based teacher standards. Surrounding student learning in two concentric circles are the eight standards for ESL/EFL teachers of adults. These standards support and sustain student learning. *Planning, Instructing,* and *Assessing* are the first three standards in the middle circle, defining teacher practices. *Planning* is the way in which a teacher plans for, adjusts, and follows up on instruction.

Figure 1. Model of Standards for ESL/EFL Teachers of Adults

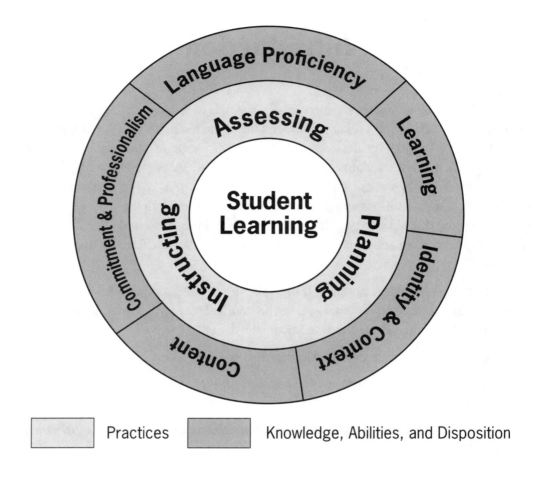

Instructing is what teachers do in a classroom setting. *Assessing* is the way in which a teacher uses knowledge and student performance to make a decision for future planning and instruction.

The outer circle contains five standards defining teacher knowledge, abilities, and disposition: *Identity and Context, Language Proficiency, Learning, Content,* and *Commitment and Professionalism. Identity and Context* focuses on who the learners are and how their communities, backgrounds, and goals shape their learning. Also included in this standard are sociocultural and sociopolitical environments that create and influence identity and, therefore, learning. *Language Proficiency* refers to an understanding of what language is and how it is used. *Learning* addresses an understanding of the learning process in formal and informal settings and the specific requirements and role of language in that process. *Content* refers to the teacher having content expertise, knowing how to collaborate with content-area teachers, or being able to facilitate the independent learning of content. *Commitment and Professionalism* focuses on the nature of ESL and EFL teaching as part of, and in relation to, the community: the teaching community at large and the community of English language teaching professionals. Collectively, these eight standards represent the core of what professional teachers of ESL and EFL to adult learners should know and be able to do.

Organization of Standards in This Book

The purpose of this book is to present the eight standards for ESL/EFL teachers of adults in a useful and concrete way, by providing examples and discussion prompts to address issues and stimulate thought. Each section has the same format:

1. title of the standard and a brief description

2. extended narrative, which elaborates the standard's theoretical justification

3. performance indicators that describe mastery of the standard; each numbered for easy identification

4. vignettes showing a clear example of many of the performance indicators in each setting

5. forum for discussion, including

   - a comprehension question that offers the reader an opportunity to return to the indicators and the vignette in order to identify key issues

   - discussion questions that are open ended and provide stimulus for thought about the vignettes, performance indicators, and the standard itself

   - a final application question

The volume concludes with a glossary and three appendixes:

- Appendix A: papers written by TESOL experts that were influential in the development of the standards

- Appendix B: performance criteria (the indicators) presented in order to facilitate program development, teacher hiring, self-review, and teacher-training programs

- Appendix C: resources and additional reading

Who Should Use This Book

The standards for ESL/EFL teachers of adults have been developed to describe effective teaching and can be applied to most settings with adult English as a second language or foreign language learners. The standards address the most important aspects of instruction and teacher performance and can benefit educators and administrators in a variety of settings.

- **Teacher-training programs** communicate the basic principles of language teaching, inspire a commitment to teaching, and model professionalism. Teacher-training programs can structure their curricula around the standards, which offer opportunities for classroom discussion and exposure to different teaching environments to inform prospective teachers' career choices. Students in teacher-training programs should understand and regularly apply the standards because educational institutions may also use the standards to evaluate faculty.

- **Educational institutions** with ESL programs will benefit from the extensive research, discussion, and feedback about effective teaching and student learning that resulted in the standards. Educational institutions may also choose to use the standards in hiring decisions, and both the standards and performance criteria (Appendix B) in teacher review policies.

The standards also address how institutions and individuals can achieve personal goals.

- **Institutional professional development** has been streamlined because of shrinking funding in the United States. Nevertheless, with special attention to Commitment and Professionalism (Standard 8), institutions can develop productive coaching relationships to improve instruction and student performance.

- **Personal professional improvement** results from a commitment to students and the acknowledgment that there is room for improvement at every stage of a person's career. The vignettes and the Performance Criteria in Appendix B can facilitate self-evaluation and re-energize experienced instructors.

Special Note

Teachers may not meet every performance indicator listed with each standard. Applying principles in the classroom leads to effective instruction, but dedication and time are also essential components. Administrators should recall this when hiring new teachers, and should acknowledge commitment and professionalism when evaluating performance. The standards for ESL/EFL teachers of adults are not meant to be discrete assessments that underscore shortcomings, but are meant to help teachers and administrators identify and develop elements of effective instruction.

References

Darling-Hammond, L., Diez, M. E., Moss, P., Pecheone, R., Pullin, D., Schafer, W. D., & Vickers, L. (1998). The role of standards and assessment: A dialogue. In M. E. Diez (Ed.), *Changing the practice of teacher education: Standards and assessment as a lever for change* (pp. 11–38). Washington, DC: American Association of Colleges for Teacher Education.

Diez, M. E. (Ed.). (1998). *Changing the practice of teacher education. Standards and assessment as a lever for change.* Washington, DC: American Association for Colleges for Teacher Education.

INTASC (Interstate New Teacher Assessment and Support Consortium). (2001). Accessed June 17, 2008, from http://www.ccsso.org/Projects/interstate_new_teacher_assessment_and_support_consortium/

Standard 1 Planning

Standard 1: Planning

Standard 1
Planning

*Teachers plan instruction to promote learning
and meet learner goals, and modify plans to
assure learner engagement and achievement.*

Teachers must be able to plan lessons and curriculum to facilitate language learning. Teachers of adults teach varied content, depending on the context of the program. For example, in U.S survival programs, teachers help learners navigate in social situations such as public transportation. In workplace settings, teachers help learners acquire vocational knowledge and learn how to use language in that environment. In academic settings, teachers help learners improve writing skills for college.

Teachers must be able to plan instruction that takes into account students' backgrounds, prior knowledge, and current interests. Teachers must plan for both long- and short-term learning goals and include in that planning a repertoire of instructional strategies to address individual learner difference. Teachers must be able to identify what learners already know and do not know in order to be able to plan lessons that meet learner needs.

When learning goals are met, teachers must be able to make decisions quickly about how to adjust instruction that fosters ongoing learning. Teachers must anticipate and value meaningful deviations for a teaching plan to meet student goals. When a student meets current learning goals, the teacher must develop new learning goals. To help students achieve learning goals, teachers must develop additional activities that encourage learners to use English and content knowledge beyond the classroom.

Standard 1: Planning
Performance Indicators

1:1 Overall Planning

- identifies and articulates short- and long-term plans to promote learning
- identifies and articulates learning goals for both language and other content

1:2 Learner Considerations

- identifies learners' interests and integrates in planning
- identifies learners' needs and integrates in planning
- identifies learners' prior learning and background knowledge and integrates in planning

1:3 Lesson Planning

- develops lesson plans that allow time for learning, review, and assessment
- develops lesson plans that include assessments to evaluate learning and achievement of objectives
- develops lesson plans that connect individual lessons to curriculum and to program objectives

1:4 Activities and Strategies

- designs or sequences strategies and activities to deliver content
- designs or sequences strategies and activities to address individual differences
- designs or sequences strategies and activities to accomplish learning objectives
- designs or sequences strategies and activities that build on learners' problem-solving and critical-thinking skills
- designs or sequences strategies and activities that employ more than one variety of English
- designs or sequences strategies and activities that encourage learners to use English beyond the classroom

1:5 Resources

- selects appropriate resources

Vignette: Adult/Community

Standard 1: Planning

Background

This vignette describes the experience of Susan Jacobson, who teaches a beginning-high English as a second language (ESL) class in a large adult education program in Southern California, and the process that she follows to develop plans for instruction. The instructor works part time in this program in the evening. She is a full-time high school English teacher during the day. She has been teaching for 5 years. The instructor has a bachelor's degree in English and a single-subject teaching credential.

The beginning-high ESL class meets three evenings a week for 2 hours each time. The program supports an open-entry, open-exit format, which allows students to enter or leave the program at any time during the 16-week term. The students are placed through a standardized test and advance from level to level after taking a state-approved standardized test and by recommendation of the instructor, who incorporates multiple measures.

There are approximately 35 students in the class. Students do not pay for instruction and have the option of buying textbooks for the class. The class consists of students from five different countries: 20 from Mexico or South American countries, 8 from Vietnam, 3 from Korea, 2 from Japan, and 2 from the Middle East. The students are immigrants, and most have been in the United States for less than 5 years. Only six students have a high school diploma earned in their country of origin. On the average, students have 6 years of formal education.

Vignette

At the beginning of the semester, Susan Jacobson maps out the term to make sure she will have time to teach what is expected of her in the program. She lists the objectives, or what she expects students to be able to do, by the end of each week, and sketches out what she *might* teach each day of class instruction. She consults the school curriculum, the standards established by the state, and the standards set forth by the organization Teachers of English to Speakers of Other Languages, Inc. (TESOL). This is the third time she has taught this level, so she will also draw from her past experience; however, she has realized over the past several years in planning that the class this term may be significantly different from the previous ones. She has learned to be flexible in this early planning because every class is different and comes with different needs and abilities. She knows that she will need to make adjustments, excluding some material that students do not need in favor of additional instruction in areas where students need more attention.

| 1:1 Overall Planning |
| 1:2 Learner Considerations |

In the 8th week of instruction, Susan is planning a new unit. The class has just completed a unit on housing. For the next 2 weeks, class instruction will focus on a community theme. Susan has learned a great deal in the last several weeks about her students. She performed a brief needs assessment on the first days of instruction and found that students were familiar with bus schedules and getting around town but had trouble asking for and giving directions

| 1:1 Overall Planning |
| 1:2 Learner Considerations |

when they did not have specific information. In the needs assessment, many students said they knew where the supermarket was but had never been in a bank or a post office. During the first 7 weeks of instruction, Susan observed that a significant number of students were reluctant to communicate with students from other cultures. Her concern prompted her to incorporate instruction early on that would prompt students to share personal information and work in teams or groups on tasks that would promote more discussion among members. Finally, she noted that students would need as many opportunities as possible to resolve problems and be challenged to think. Linguistically, the students were extremely diverse. Several students had command of writing, and several had limited literacy skills. She knew, even before working with these particular students, that she would need to plan a variety of activities each class period that would address different learning styles and, as often as possible, the four skill areas. Based on what she has learned, Susan chooses the following objectives for the six sessions she will devote to community: *identify places in the community, follow and give street directions, read a map, read a telephone directory, open a bank account,* and *send mail through the post office.* In her earlier planning she had included *reading bus schedules* but now has chosen to exclude it and instead introduce *banking.* She plans to make sure each lesson builds from the last so there is a concrete link from one lesson to the next.

Now that Susan has established which lessons she will teach, she begins to plan specifics based on what her students need. Susan has just finished the lesson on *places in the community* and now turns her attention to *following and giving street directions.* She incorporates an established lesson plan format that allows her to sequence activities in a natural progression leading to an application of the objective. She finds that the textbook has a good presentation for her purposes and, with a few adjustments, she can incorporate the sections in the book into her lesson plan. She makes sure that there is a listening component, and she decides that among the activities there should be an opportunity for students to practice critical-thinking skills in heterogeneous groups. She plans a final application activity where students in groups will write out directions from the school to an undisclosed location in the community. Then the group will share their directions with the class. The class will read the directions and guess the undisclosed location. Now that Susan has established the application, she goes back to the previous activities and refines them to ensure that students will have the tools to accomplish the final task. She reminds herself that the lesson plan might not go as planned and that she needs to be flexible enough to address student needs as they materialize. She has built into the lesson opportunities to evaluate what students already know, and she anticipates that this information will prompt adjustments. It takes Susan about 45 minutes to complete her planning for a 2-hour class. She cheerfully remembers that when she started teaching 5 years ago it took her more than 1½ hours to do the same planning.

Susan has completed the lesson on *following and giving directions.* She takes 5 minutes to record her impressions about the lesson and what she might do to improve it next time. She evaluates whether or not the students were able to do what she had planned and if all their needs were met. She realizes that if there are deficiencies, she will need to address those concerns in the warm-up and review section of the next lesson and in the next lesson itself. After this brief self-evaluation, Susan stores her lesson plan in a notebook so she can access it next time she teaches this objective. She is now ready to plan or refine the next lesson.

1:3 Lesson Planning
1:4 Activities and Strategies
1:5 Resources

1:1 Overall Planning

Discussion

A. Study the vignette. The steps Susan follows are listed below in random order. Number them in order using Susan's step-by-step approach to her planning.

> ____ Design lessons based on student needs.
>
> _1_ List possible objectives at the beginning of the term.
>
> ____ Identify student needs after extended observation.
>
> ____ Plan or refine next lesson.
>
> ____ Record impressions immediately.
>
> ____ Choose objectives for upcoming unit.

[Answer Key A: 4-1-2-6-5-3]

B. Discuss the following:

1. There are several performance indicators for Standard 1 that reveal a need to understand the student population when planning a term, lessons, and activities. Discuss in a group how and when student needs can be identified.

2. Planning must be a fluid and flexible process. Discuss how flexibility is incorporated into Susan's planning.

C. Make a list of techniques that you might try to better identify and address student needs.

Vignette: Workplace

Standard 1: Planning

Background

This vignette describes the planning processes of a work-based program. The development of this program started with a phone call from an asbestos removal company to the community education department at a community college located in Memphis, Tennessee. Recently, the college has been marketing services to local businesses with increasingly large numbers of employees who are nonnative speakers of English. Sandra St. Paul, the chair of the department, first meets several times with the asbestos removal company in order to determine need and to start the planning process for teaching employees at this company.

Sandra and the owner of the company agree that the class will consist of 12 ESL students, 10 men and 2 women. Nine workers are native speakers of Spanish from South and Central American countries, two are speakers of Arabic, and one is from Somalia and speaks Somali and some Arabic. The education level of the trainees varies, but all trainees have some education in their native language and minimal conversation skills in English. These workers have all been through the standard training program for asbestos abatement, which consists primarily of lecture supplemented by slides and visual aids. However, the supervisors have indicated that these workers do not seem to be familiar with the required procedures. The workers in question are making mistakes in the field and having difficulty following the procedures, and these problems have been attributed to their limited English proficiency.

The owner is concerned about his workers' health and their compliance with industry safety standards. He agrees to provide opportunities for students to take classes during the trainees' normal work hours, 2-hour classes 3 days a week for 10 weeks.

The teacher for this class is Marjorie Lloyd. She holds a master's degree in TESOL, and has had more than 10 years of experience teaching ESL and more than 2 years teaching work-based programs.

Vignette

1:2 Learner Considerations

The community college sends out a team to do a 2-day needs analysis. The team goes to an asbestos removal site and to the company headquarters to observe and document the communication needs of the job, the types of tasks the trainees have to perform, the interactions between the supervisors and workers, and all interactions among workers. Marjorie Lloyd, the instructor chosen for this assignment, also interviews the owner to find out if there will be changes related to equipment, regulations, standards, or processes in the next few years.

1:1 Overall Planning
1:5 Resources

From the observations and documentation collected, the team creates a syllabus, which includes checklists of specific goals and objectives, benchmarks with estimated completion dates, and assessment tools for the course. The syllabus also includes samples of industry-specific terms, equipment, manuals, safety standards, and forms that Marjorie and her team need in order to customize the course with authentic materials as often as possible. The team then develops the curriculum, workbooks, and assessment tools.

At a meeting to discuss the needs analysis, Marjorie helps the owner understand what can be expected during the training by sharing three benchmarks with objectives and probable dates for completion. She agrees to provide reports after completing each of the three stages of training. The reports will include an overall view of achievements, assessments, and surveys. A final report will explain the failures, successes, and recommendations for individual trainees and the group as a whole. Marjorie and the owner agree that each trainee will receive a workbook with information about course objectives. Each trainee will also receive an individual report at each reporting date that includes a copy of his or her graded folder.

1:1 Overall
Planning

As a team, the college representatives and the owner plan out the specific length and structure of the program. They agree upon a standardized test, as a measure of their beginning and ending communication skills. Marjorie also explains that the students will be given reading, writing, speaking, and listening tests throughout the program. Marjorie will use the results of these assessments for further planning and as part of the trainee portfolio for each student that she will provide. This information will also be used to improve the course in the future.

1:1 Overall
Planning

Marjorie plans that 15 minutes of each class will address other needs the trainees may have outside of the work environment. She states that satisfying these needs will enhance the students' interest in attending the course and will improve their cultural knowledge and language ability. The needs analysis indicates that the workers need to be able to identify and discuss the various pieces of equipment, to understand instructions given by the supervisor, to take part in problem solving, to make suggestions for better processes, to keep coworkers informed about progress on the tasks they are assigned, and to interact both socially and in work-related situations with their fellow colleagues.

1:2 Learner
Considerations

After meeting with a focus group with other employees and supervisors, Marjorie decides to give more emphases to specific language that is required in particular settings. Based on the recommendations of the focus group, she also decides to include a series of sessions on health risks and cultural differences. Marjorie decides to include several role-plays in the class experience to help students prepare for discussions outside of class. The role-plays will include topics about setting up, working in, and cleaning up asbestos work sites. They include explanations lasting between 30 seconds and 1 minute about the equipment, procedures, and even problems with coworkers. Instruction will include lists of work-related idioms, acronyms, industry-specific vocabulary, and basic subjects for small talk. Lists of language functions and settings have also been developed into checklists. The checklists make it easy to develop scenarios for work tasks and small talk, and to meet the language objectives of the course.

1:3 Lesson
Planning

1:5 Resources

Marjorie's final list of goals, objectives, and benchmarks for the students includes measurable outcomes such as the ability to indicate lack of comprehension and seek clarification, to identify equipment by the formal and common names, to describe work procedures, to understand instructions for specific tasks, and to understand consequences of not following procedures, especially those for safety. She has other goals for the class that are harder to measure, including increasing the willingness of the workers to ask questions and express concerns, but she hopes to address those issues through problem-solving and role-playing activities. These goals drive her lesson planning.

1:1 Overall
Planning

Once a week Marjorie plans out the next week's activities based on what she has learned in the previous week. She realizes that a good sequence of activities will yield the most student success. She allows 15 minutes for students to voice concerns and issues at the start of each class, after which there will be a presentation based on the established objectives. The presentation will include the work-specific vocabulary and settings common to the workplace. Most often the students will perform role-plays or written tasks based on existing forms following the presentations to practice the new information. After the role-plays or writing tasks, Marjorie plans on providing students with opportunities to work in teams on projects such as developing ideas to improve processes or to better understand them. Marjorie sees this last type of activity as an essential form of application that will motivate students to participate in work-related issues outside of class.

During the course Marjorie learns that many of the ESL workers expect their jobs to be temporary, and have long-term goals of getting training in a technical field or getting jobs in construction. She also learns that two workers plan to work for the asbestos abatement company only long enough to save some money and then return to their home countries. Marjorie searches for ways to motivate them. She plans to ensure that all the workers, and especially those who do not plan to stay, understand the harm they could cause themselves and their friends and families if they don't follow the safety procedures for dealing with asbestos. She adjusts her lessons to emphasize safety concerns.

In the 15 minutes they spend in every class discussing needs, the trainees request information about dealing with institutions such as the post office and banks in the United States. As a result, Marjorie plans to include additional background information and role-playing about some common situations. She also plans to add role-plays that are useful in both the workplace and everyday life, such as going to lunch with an English-speaking colleague, declining an invitation, and making a reservation.

Discussion

A. Study the vignette. Match the discussion activity with one of the topics in the right column. Write the appropriate letter in the left column.

	Discussion Activity	Discussion Topic
	Observation of the workplace	a. trainee concerns
	Discussion with management	b. needs analysis
	Focus group with coworkers and supervisors	c. length and structure of program
	Discussion with student during the course	d. cultural issues

[Answer Key A: b-c-d-a]

B. Discuss the following:

1. Who should take part in the needs-analysis process in a workplace setting?

2. Describe a role-playing or problem-solving activity that Marjorie might use in this course. Which of her goals would your activity address? How could your activity be used for assessment as well as instruction?

C. Ideally, what activities should be undertaken to do a thorough needs analysis before designing the curriculum for a workplace program? Who should be involved in making decisions?

Vignette: College/University

Standard 1: Planning

Background

This vignette describes the long- and short-term planning of a lecturer in a 3-credit advanced ESL composition class in a northern Midwest public university. The class consists of 23 sophomores and juniors, mostly international students and some immigrants, from Asia, Central America, Europe, and Africa. Students are admitted to this course, the highest in the ESL program, by performance on the placement exam or by completion of the prerequisite composition class. The primary goal of the program is to support the academic literacy needs of students who are currently enrolled in academic courses.

Matt Jorgensen has been teaching at the university for about 5 years and had previously taught in Japan and traveled extensively in Asia. He teaches four classes at the university, usually two sections of composition and two sections of listening/speaking. After 4 years of teaching, he decided to change to the sustained content approach, an approach used in both first and second language instruction in which one topic is used throughout a course. He was enthusiastic about the possibility of leading students to deeper levels of analysis and understanding by getting them to read, think, and write about issues related to a single topic, rather than jumping from topic to topic.

Vignette

In planning the revised course, Matt decides to use a nonfiction book, Anne Fadiman's *The Spirit Catches You and You Fall Down: A Hmong Child, Her American Doctors, and the Collision of Two Cultures,* because of the engaging story, excellent writing, and variety of social, cultural, and political issues it raises. He reviews his plans with the program coordinator, making it clear that he will be able to meet the current course objectives with this approach. The objectives for students include writing four essays; learning about online databases; using appropriate outside sources in papers; analyzing and writing argumentative essays; refining skills in paraphrasing, summarizing, and citing sources; improving critical reading and annotating; keeping double-entry reading journals; taking in-class writing exams; and participating in a course Web site for discussion. He also has enlisted a colleague to try out this approach with him so that they can share materials and see how the approach works with different classes and instructors. He and his colleague do some general planning together, such as mapping out the objectives of the four units on a weekly basis, setting the due dates of the papers and exams, and figuring out how to pace the 19 chapters of the book.

1:5 Resources

As part of the course, Matt and his colleague agree that they need new course readings to go with topics pertinent to the book (e.g., parents' rights, U.S. medical care, refugees, and foster care). They identify the central topics, and each finds two readings and prepares worksheets to aid comprehension, analysis, and reflection. Matt also plans and revises handouts for the course so the examples in these materials match the new topics. The only other text for the course is a handbook for writers. He puts the readings and other new materials in a course reader that the students could purchase at the bookstore. Matt needs to complete this step before the start of the semester because he knows that once he starts teaching, he will have little spare time for materials development.

While teaching a class, however, Matt regularly selects and uses current student writing as models, so he realizes he will have to do this as the course unfolds. He is pleased that he and his colleague can share in this task. In order to provide additional interest and cultural information to the course, and to provide for the varied learning styles of the students, Matt wants to include some films. He searches the university's audiovisual collection and finds two short documentary films to show in class (one on the migration of Southeast Asians and another on shamanic rituals). Finally, he and his colleague discuss whether to provide comprehension questions for each chapter of the book; they realize that they do not have time to prepare the questions, so they brainstorm an alternative way to process the readings: have the students talk about the chapter in groups, put ideas on the board from their double-entry reading journals, and lead the discussions. Matt decides that if the students need more guidance, he can always prepare a few questions for each chapter at the last minute and lead the discussions himself, as he traditionally has done in the past.

> 1:2 Learner Considerations
> 1:5 Resources

During the semester, Matt makes adjustments based on his students' performance and interests. For example, two of the readings were especially difficult for the class, partly because they had no background knowledge of the topic, so he had to add some schema-building mini-lectures (3–5 minutes) to help students with comprehension. He also learned that several of the students were interested in topics that he had not predicted (such as the "dirty" war in Laos and faith healing versus western medicine), so he decides to add two more articles to help these students benefit from the reading and discussion like their classmates. This work used class time that he had not built into the schedule, so he compensated by devoting less class time to these readings and allowing for further discussion on the course Web site. Fortunately, students were not having trouble citing sources, and Matt was able to move quickly through that material. To his great relief, the new approach to processing the book chapters was successful: Students enthusiastically led class discussions on the content and their reflections, and Matt could see in student journals that the class was stimulated by the book and readily able to comprehend it.

> 1:2 Learner Considerations
> 1:3 Lesson Planning
> 1:4 Activities and Strategies

In evaluating Semester 1, Matt and his colleague agreed (and student evaluations confirmed) that the book and its content were successful at engaging the students in the narrative, the characters, and the related topics, and at getting them to think, read, and write more seriously and critically about the issues raised by the text. For example, when they wrote their second paper, many students expressed the view (based on their cultural experience) that the parents' rights were of paramount importance; after reading about the ethics of medical care and patients' rights and about the foster care system (and having a class debate on the issues), they were able to question their own beliefs and see the complexities of the situation, and then cite relevant evidence supporting varied perspectives. Thus, Matt's hard work in planning the revised course had paid off; he had satisfied his goal by switching to a sustained content approach.

> 1:1 Overall Planning

There is more work to be done, however: Matt must find replacement readings for the ones that seemed too complex, rework the class lesson plans and schedule so that he can have more than four readings, prepare his mini-lectures more thoroughly, and add other samples of student writing (from the Semester 1 class) to the course materials. Finally, by listening to his students and reading their papers and journals over the course of the semester, Matt feels much more prepared to teach the course again and is more equipped to anticipate student interests and to adjust for the varied abilities of a class.

Discussion

A. Study the vignette and identify ways in which Matt's planning reflects his desire to

 1. address learner needs and interests

 2. select appropriate resources that take individual differences into account

 3. design activities that use and build on learners' problem-solving and critical-thinking skills

 4. connect lessons to course and program objectives

 5. adjust instruction based on student progress and feedback

 [Answer Key A: Answers will vary: 1, 2: chooses films, adds mini-lectures, adds articles based on student interests; 3: provides activities that allow for open-ended discussions; 4: identifies objectives, creates worksheets, and rewrites existing handouts to match topics; 5: adds articles and online discussion time]

B. Discuss the following:

 1. Matt's planning for restructuring his course was based on one global objective that he felt the course was not addressing successfully: the depth of students' critical reading, thinking, and writing skills. Given that his course has to cover many writing skills in addition to this critical-thinking component, do you think that student learning increased enough to justify the time and effort he put into the new course? Why or why not?

 2. Describe how Matt's ability to collaborate with a colleague aided his planning and implementation of the course. Discuss experiences you have had collaborating with your colleagues on long- and short-term planning of courses or units. What are some advantages and disadvantages of a collaborative approach to planning?

C. Describe an instance in which you had to plan a change in one of your courses at any level from a major change like Matt's to a momentary change in the middle of a class session. On what basis did you make this change? What was the outcome?

Vignette: Intensive English

Standard 1: Planning

Background

This vignette describes the instructional planning process used by an instructor who teaches a low-advanced class in an intensive English program (IEP) housed in a large private university in Wisconsin. This instructor, Karen Peterson, has a master's degree in TESOL and has been teaching full time in this program for 7 years. Prior to joining the program, she taught in Japan for 2 years.

The primary mission of the program is to prepare international students for degree programs at American universities, so it focuses on English for academic purposes (EAP). The program teaches an average of 120 students per quarter and has a staff of approximately 15 instructors, 11 of whom are full time. It provides 18–24 hours per week of study in six levels of instruction.

Most of the students in this program are international students studying full time on student visas. This particular class has 14 students, 12 of whom are from Asia (3 from South Korea, 4 from Japan, 3 from Thailand, and 2 from Taiwan), and 2 are from the Middle East (Kuwait and Saudi Arabia). Ten students are seeking undergraduate degrees, and four are seeking graduate degrees, mostly in engineering and business.

Vignette

Prior to the beginning of the term, Karen meets with her colleagues who teach the low-advanced level. She will be teaching the listening/speaking course, which meets for 6 hours weekly. The other instructors will teach reading/writing (6 hours weekly), grammar (3 hours weekly), and several elective courses such as pronunciation and TOEFL (Test of English as a Foreign Language) preparation. Since the listening/speaking and reading/writing courses are theme-based, the instructors coordinate the topics to be covered in the courses and the timing of assignments. They also discuss possible ways to integrate instruction across courses. One of the instructional units they plan together will focus on the theme *skills for college success*. As part of the unit, Karen will invite three of the campus counselors to deliver lectures to her class on the topics of time management, study strategies, and stress management. The reading/writing instructor will assign a research paper on the same theme. This unit reflects the overall philosophy of the program, which attempts to integrate relevant academic content for college-bound students with practice in language.

> 1:1 Overall Planning
> 1:5 Resources

After meeting with her colleagues, Karen prepares her own course syllabus, which outlines weekly tasks and major assignments. This is the third time she has taught this course, so she plans several activities that have been successful in the past. Karen is excited because she is adopting a new textbook this term, and the book includes radio interviews on global topics that she believes will be very appealing to the students. Karen thinks this text will be much better than the one she previously used. The former text was based on a series of academic lectures produced for the textbook, which Karen found somewhat contrived and artificial. Karen hopes

> 1:5 Resources

that this new textbook will expose the students to more natural and colloquial forms of the language. She also plans to use other authentic resources to supplement the textbook, such as videos from the school library and radio programs that can be accessed on the Internet.

1:2 Learner Considerations

In week 6 of the term, Karen is preparing to introduce the unit on *skills for college success.* By now Karen knows her students well. The diagnostic test she administered at the beginning of the term revealed that these particular students' listening and note-taking skills are quite strong, but most of them need more practice in spoken English. Therefore, Karen has decided to add several oral activities to her original syllabus, and to exclude some short listening tasks that she had planned to use. Karen is now aware of her individual students' strengths and weaknesses, so she groups students in a way that allows them to help each other.

1:3 Lesson Planning

1:4 Activities and Strategies

When planning the first few lessons for the unit, Karen uses the textbook chapter on test anxiety to introduce the theme and to prepare the students for the upcoming lectures by the guest speakers. Before starting the unit, Karen plans to conduct a whole-class discussion that draws on the students' former academic experiences in high school and college. Together, the students will brainstorm a list of important academic skills and comment on their own strengths and weaknesses. This discussion will serve several purposes: For the students, it will activate background knowledge on the topic, introduce important vocabulary, and help them start to identify topics for the unit's culminating activity (a survey of domestic students followed by an oral in-class presentation). For Karen, it will allow her to identify vocabulary that students already know and that they need to learn to complete the tasks ahead.

1:3 Lesson Planning

1:4 Activities and Strategies

After this discussion, Karen plans to use the activities in the textbook for the next few lessons. The prelistening activities include vocabulary exercises and a questionnaire about test anxiety. The main task in the chapter consists of a radio interview with a college student who describes his experiences overcoming test anxiety. The interview is divided into three parts, with comprehension checks throughout. Karen estimates that it will take her approximately three classes to do the introductory discussion and finish the listening activities in the textbook.

Meanwhile, Karen is planning for the rest of the unit's activities. She has set up meetings with each guest speaker to discuss the content of the lectures so she can plan prelecture activities and postlecture assessments. She has also contacted three students who will need extra help with the culminating activity. This activity will require them to interview domestic students about their academic struggles and to present the results of these interviews in class. Karen knows that these three students will benefit from meeting with her individually before the interviews to clarify the questions and, afterwards, to discuss how to organize and present the information.

1:4 Activities and Strategies

Karen plans to assess her students' performance in several ways. She will conduct informal assessments throughout the unit by observing the students as they complete classroom tasks (e.g., listening comprehension questions, note-taking during lectures). She will grade each student's oral presentation of interview results based on a rubric that includes content, organization, and language use. Finally, she will give a test at the end of the unit with questions covering the content and vocabulary from the lectures.

Discussion

A. Read the vignette. In planning her course, Karen carefully thinks about long- and short-term goals. Find examples of each.

   1. Long-term goals:

   2. Short-term goals:

   [Answer Key A: 1. Answers include planning out the whole course, topics, and objectives. 2. Answers include planning out unit objectives just previous to starting it and planning a few lessons ahead.]

B. Discuss the following:

   1. Discuss at least three ways in which Karen considers her students' needs in planning her course.

   2. How does Karen plan to encourage her students to use English beyond the classroom?

C. Make a list of other tasks you might assign to encourage your learners to use English outside the classroom.

Vignette: English as a Foreign Language

Standard 1: Planning

Background

This vignette describes the instructional planning by an instructor who teaches for a private language school in Rio de Janeiro, Brazil. The school has been contracted by the local branch of a large international bank to provide English language classes for its employees. The instructor, Ana Ribeiro, has a bachelor's degree in English and has been teaching full time for this school for 3 years. This particular class is offered on site at the bank's downtown office. The students, a group of eight Brazilian middle-level managers from several different departments within the bank, all speak a little English. They meet in their conference room twice a week during their lunch hour to attend Ana's class. Ana has been teaching groups like this one for almost a year.

Vignette

1:1 Overall
Planning

1:2 Learner
Considerations

Ana first meets with the group at the beginning of the year and spends the first week assessing her students' level of English as well as their needs and possible objectives. She performs this assessment through a conversation with the group. The students take turns telling Ana about their daily activities at work. Ana then asks them to write short essays describing their goals for the class. She also asks them to provide a self-assessment of their strengths and weaknesses in the four language skills.

1:2 Learner
Considerations

From the conversation, the essay, and the self-assessment, Ana is able to assess the students' language levels. She concludes that six of them are high intermediate, one is low intermediate, and one is advanced. Ana also finds that three of her students take frequent business trips to the bank's branch offices in different European cities. The other students in the class do not travel as much; however, they interact regularly with bank employees from other countries who come to visit Brazil. All these interactions are conducted in English. The students tell Ana that their primary goal is to develop fluency in oral communication. Only two of the eight students express a desire to work on reading and writing skills, mainly for the purpose of e-mail correspondence. The group agrees that the classes will focus primarily on speaking and listening skills.

1:3 Lesson
Planning

1:4 Activities
and Strategies

1:5 Resources

The school has adopted a textbook and video series focusing on English for business, and it requires that all instructors teaching the business courses use these materials. The textbook and accompanying video follow a situational approach and include units on topics such as running a meeting, negotiating a contract, and interviewing someone for a job. Each unit presents realistic scenarios and dialogues that simulate situations her students are likely to encounter in their professional interactions, so Ana thinks these resources will be very useful for her students.

She chooses the intermediate volume of the series for the group, and starts using it during the second week. In class, she focuses mostly on the listening and speaking activities provided in each unit. For the two students who want to work on reading and writing skills, she assigns the reading sections for homework. To check their understanding of the readings and to develop their writing skills, Ana exchanges e-mail messages with these two students on a weekly basis.

During the first month of the course, Ana follows the textbook exclusively. The students seem to be making good progress on their use of business-related English. However, they start to express frustrations about difficulties carrying out informal conversations with business partners. Ana comes to realize that her students need to develop oral fluency in general English communication in addition to working on business-related language. Based on this feedback, Ana decides to bring in supplementary resources to enrich her classes, such as videotaped news reports, newspaper articles, and other authentic resources found on the Internet, such as advertisements and weather reports.

1:2 Learner Considerations
1:5 Resources

Because the class meets twice a week, Ana develops a plan to work once a week on English for business, using the textbook and materials adopted by her school, and once a week on English for general communication, using resources she develops on her own. She continues to assign weekly readings and to engage in e-mail dialogues with the two students who want to develop written skills.

1:5 Resources

When planning a class for the following week, Ana focuses on a recent news report about Brazil's decision to cut ties with the International Monetary Fund (IMF). This is a high-interest topic for her students, who are all bank employees. In order to prepare for her lesson, Ana records a 5-minute newscast from CNN on this topic. She then accesses the CNN Web site to obtain the transcript of the video segment. She also reads several Internet pieces on this topic and selects a short article to assign to the two students as homework.

1:5 Resources

After collecting and studying all these materials, Ana starts preparing her lesson. She will start the class by showing the group the first few minutes of the video. Then she will pause the newscast and ask the students some general questions about the functions of the IMF and Brazil's past relationship with the agency. She knows that her students will have strong opinions about whether or not the Brazilian government has made a good decision, but she will ask them to save those opinions for later. For the moment, her objective will be to focus on factual information to aid the group's comprehension of the video segment. After the initial discussion, she will show the whole video to the students. She prepares a handout with comprehension questions for the students to fill out while they watch. She plans to show the video several times while checking the comprehension questions, and to share the transcript with the students at the end.

1:3 Lesson Planning
1:4 Activities and Strategies

Ana calculates that the initial discussion and the viewing activity will last approximately 30 minutes. She plans to spend the rest of the period on a debate about the benefits and drawbacks of the Brazilian government's decision to cut ties with the IMF. She decides to do this through a simulation exercise.

1:3 Lesson Planning

Ana will divide the class into two groups and ask the class to go back in time. They are to pretend that it is the previous year. President Lula is considering the decision to cut ties with the IMF and decides to consult with two groups of advisors. One group is in favor of the decision, and the other group is against. The students' job is to convince President Ana to follow the advice of their group. Ana will give each group a few minutes to prepare their arguments, after which each group will have an opportunity to present ideas. Ana plans to videotape this simulation. As a follow-up activity at a subsequent class meeting, she will view the simulation with the class and ask the students to assess their performance.

1:4 Activities and Strategies

Discussion

A. Read the vignette carefully. Describe at least three ways in which Ana integrates her students' needs and current interests in her course and lesson planning.

[Answer Key A: Answers include preliminary group conversations, student written goals, self-assessment, e-mail exchanges, discussions, specialized instruction in reading and writing for specific students.]

B. Discuss the following:

1. Ana designs activities that encourage her students to employ more than one variety of English. Discuss the activities she plans to help her students use English in business and social situations.

   a. English for business purposes

   b. English for social purposes

2. Ana selects appropriate resources to meet her teaching objectives. List them and explain the objective(s) for each.

C. Do you have a process that you follow to determine the instructional resources that would meet the objectives of the course? Discuss one course you have given and how you identified the resources you used. Would you do anything differently the next time you teach the course?

Standard 2 Instructing

Standard 2: Instructing

Standard 2
Instructing

Teachers create supportive environments that engage all learners in purposeful learning and promote respectful classroom interactions.

Teachers must create environments (face-to-face and virtual) that engage all learners in purposeful learning, promote fairness and respect, and meet learners' goals. Because learning is an active, collaborative process of knowledge construction, teachers must organize constructive interactions among learners and between learners and teaching resources. They must manage interactions so as to encourage learners to participate in making decisions and in working both collaboratively and individually as appropriate.

Teachers must select appropriate teaching methods, make content accessible, and respond to learner questions effectively. Teachers must negotiate guidelines for a respectful and comfortable learning environment with learners. Teachers must make effective use of instructional time to promote learning. Teachers must use a variety of appropriate resources and strategies in teaching concepts. Teachers must provide opportunities for learning through problem-solving and critical-thinking activities. Teachers must help all learners gain access to useful material, resources, and technologies to support their learning of English and additional subject matter.

Standard 2: Instructing
Performance Indicators

2:1 Classroom Management

- organizes and manages constructive interactions
- creates an environment that engages all learners
- makes effective use of classroom time
- manages activities
- adjusts instruction when necessary
- uses unexpected events to extend learning

2:2 Instructor Role

- makes goals explicit
- gives clear instructions
- promotes learner participation
- listens and responds to learner talk
- models natural language use
- models and promotes respectful interactions among learners
- asks questions to check for comprehension
- facilitates discussion
- clarifies student thinking
- gives corrective feedback

2:3 Activities and Strategies

- uses a variety of strategies and activities to introduce, explain, and restate concepts and processes
- uses a variety of strategies and activities to address individual differences
- uses a variety of strategies and activities to group learners in a variety of ways to meet goals
- uses a variety of strategies and activities to make content accessible
- uses a variety of strategies and activities to further critical-thinking skills

2:4 Learner Considerations

- treats learners as adults
- conveys and maintains expectations for learner behavior
- engages learners in decision-making about their learning
- helps learners become independent, lifelong learners

Vignette: Adult/Community

Standard 2: Instructing

Background

This vignette describes the class of an instructor who teaches an intermediate-high English as a second language (ESL) class in an adult ESL program in Texas. The instructor teaches full time during the day and teaches two other ESL classes. He incorporates various instructional strategies to maximize learning.

The ESL class consists of 28 students, most of Hispanic origin. The class meets two times a week for 2 hours each day. The program supports an open-entry, open-exit format, which allows students to enter or leave the program at any time during the 20-week term. The students are placed through a standardized placement test. Students advance to the next level based on the instructors' assessment of student progress through regular activities that include student portfolios, tests, and a state-approved exam.

The lesson is based on a well-organized plan with six steps: warm-up, introduction, presentation, practice, evaluation, and application. The objective is chosen based on student needs, in this case pertaining to a unit on jobs and job-related issues. The previous lesson objective required students to read and understand classified ads. In this lesson, students learn to complete a job application. The students have limited contact hours, and the instructor recognizes the importance of identifying specific student needs early in the semester. He chooses specific objectives for a lesson based on the identified needs of a group and goals of a particular program. He is careful to make good use of class time but aware that he must sometimes adjust the focus of a lesson based on student participation.

Vignette

Pedro Herrera, the instructor, arrives 15 minutes early in order to confirm that he has all the needed resources for the class. He also writes the agenda on the board. As the students enter the classroom, he greets each one and has short conversations with a few. Since Pedro knows all the students by name, he does not take roll, but takes care of this task and other class business after class, when students have left.

2:1 Classroom Management

2:4 Learner Considerations

Warm-up (15 minutes): Pedro starts the class by putting students in groups of three or four. He distributes a handout to each group. The handouts have eight classified ads on them. He only gives one handout to each group to encourage the group members to work together. He then gives each group one of four 3 × 5 cards. Each card has personal information and the work experience of one of four prospective employees. He asks each group to identify on their 3 × 5 card which job from the classified ads would be best suited for the person, and to share their answers with the class. Students interact in their groups and present their conclusions to the class. There are at least two possible jobs for each person identified on the cards.

2:3 Activities and Strategies

2:2 Instructor Role 2:3 Activities and Strategies	Introduction (5 minutes): Pedro asks members of different groups to write the personal information from the cards on the board so all four prospective employees are represented. He then quickly role-plays a phone conversation with a student, in which the student is an employer and Pedro is a person looking for a job. He prompts the student to suggest that he come in for a job application. The student does not comply, so Pedro gives him an application form and makes sure that all the other students see what it is. Finally, with some coaxing from other students, the student suggests that he come and get an application. Then he points to the objective listed on the board and states it clearly to the students.
2:2 Instructor Role 2:4 Learner Considerations	Presentation (30 minutes): Pedro presents new material by placing a transparency of a completed job application on the board. The job application is from one of the four prospective employees. He asks questions about the information on the form: He asks who a reference should be and what possible reasons for leaving might be, and he clarifies other items on the application. As students respond, he checks off the personal information for the person who is already on the board. Pedro then puts up a new transparency of an incomplete job application for another position and asks students to complete the application on the board by using the information from another prospective employee already on the board. The student who starts writing the information about job history forgets that the information is to be in reverse-chronological order. Other students feel comfortable challenging what the student has written, and the class reviews each portion of the application. Finally, to be sure students have a good grasp of the concepts, Pedro quizzes them orally on definitions of terms on the application. He gives the following definition, for example: *This is the person who checked your work in your last job.* Students look at each other and one finally replies: *supervisor.*
2:3 Activities and Strategies 2:4 Learner Considerations	Practice 1 (10 minutes): Pedro passes out an application form to pairs of students. The form includes minimal information about another prospective employee on the board. Pedro asks students in pairs to complete the form. As they work, he walks around and monitors the progress. When he notices students speaking in Spanish and straying from the task, he walks over and addresses them in English. He asks them questions about the task and redirects them to focus on the work. He asks them if they would be willing to share their completed form with the class at the end of the task. The students agree and share their work.
2:2 Instructor Role 2:3 Activities and Strategies	Practice 2 (15 minutes): Pedro passes out another application form with minimal information about the fourth prospective employee on the board. He asks that the pairs situate themselves in the room so that one of them can see the board and the other cannot. He asks the students who cannot see the board to complete the form by asking for information from the students who can see the board. Then the pairs check their answers. During the activity, Pedro sees many capitalization and spelling errors. He stops the group to do an impromptu mini-presentation in which he stresses the importance of accuracy. He does this by asking them to imagine how an employer who received 100 applications might eliminate candidates.
2:2 Instructor Role	Evaluation (15 minutes): Pedro has been observing the students throughout the class and believes that they are ready for the application. To test his hypothesis, he orally quizzes students and is pleased with the results. Pedro reminds the students about the objective of the class and asks them if they are ready to complete their own application. Some students protest because they do not have the information they need, but Pedro assures them that they can do much of the work in class and finish the task for homework.

Application (15 minutes): Pedro reminds the class that this is a real-world activity, and that they can use the form they will complete as a model when they are looking for a job. He also tells the class that they will use their completed application in the next lesson on interviewing skills. Students are given two blank applications, one to complete in pencil as a practice exercise and the other to be done as accurately as possible in ink. Pedro gently corrects students as needed while they work on the application until the end of class.

2:2 Instructor Role

2:3 Activities and Strategies

2:4 Learner Considerations

Discussion

A. Study the vignette. Instructors use many different approaches to lesson planning. Pedro chooses a six-step approach. Below are the characteristics of the six steps in random order. Label the steps using the following labels: warm-up/review, introduction, presentation, practice, evaluation, and application.

_____ Focus student attention on the lesson and state the objective.

_____ Introduce new information and prepare for practice.

_____ Begin a lesson with information from a previous lesson.

_____ Students do an activity where they take ownership.

_____ Have students practice new knowledge.

_____ Evaluate student attainment of the objective.

[Answer Key A: introduction, presentation, warm-up/review, application, practice, and evaluation]

B. Discuss the following:

1. There are a few instances when Pedro's lesson did not go as planned. What adjustments did Pedro make to compensate?

2. Encouraging student participation is one of the performance indicators. Did Pedro include all students? Did he do anything to encourage participation? If so, what did he do?

C. Make a list of other techniques you might choose to involve your students.

Vignette: Workplace

Standard 2: Instructing

Background

A large U.S. multinational telemarketing organization has opened an India branch call center. The India branch hires only English-speaking job candidates. The organization has provided their workers, or agents, substantial amounts of product training. Because all the agents had at least 8 years of English instruction in school, they have received very little training in language and communication skills. Most of the agents have U.S. accents. However, after a short time on the phones, these agents have been identified as having language problems because they are unable to deal appropriately in English with their customers. The organization's supervisors, although subject experts, have little cross-cultural or teaching experience. An English language instructor has been called in to help. The instructional design of the approach is an intensive series of coaching classes during which the English language instructor works collaboratively with the supervisors and agents to provide small-group training and coaching. Through this training, the supervisors become coaches. The instructor is highly qualified, with more than 10 years of experience teaching in workplace settings. The coaches select 12 agents to participate. Coaches receive 3 hours of instructional training per week related to the agent's training tasks. Coaching techniques are discussed, modeled, and practiced. The instructor and the coach review the previous week's training and coaching sessions.

Groups of four agents meet with the instructor and each of the organization's supervisors (coaches). Each group of agents participates in 2 hours of classes, three times a week with the coach and the instructor. Coaching is available for 1 hour at the beginning of each shift. The coaching is always taped or filmed and reviewed by the instructor, who then reviews the session with the coach so the supervisor can improve his or her training skills.

The coaching session includes 1 hour of intensive on-the-job training by the supervisor. The agent takes calls as usual, and the coach listens to the call with a headset that plugs into the phone. The coach notes communication problems and then provides feedback to the agent immediately after each call. After this practice, the agent is debriefed and continues to work undisturbed for the rest of the shift.

Vignette

2:1 Classroom Management

The instructor, John Hildebrand, has been given a small room where he can meet with the coaches and the agents after their shifts. He arrives early in order to set up the area for the class. As the agents and coaches enter, he talks to them about their experiences that day and puts them at ease by promoting a friendly and warm environment. He first notices that the coaches and agents are sitting separately, and he encourages them to sit in groups so agents and coaches are mingled throughout the small classroom.

Warm-up (10 minutes): John plays a recording from the previous week's videos and shows students how they have improved. He asks students to talk to coaches next to them and to discuss briefly the experiences they had that day. He asks them to share one positive experience and a challenge they may have had.

Review (20 minutes): John reviews the homework with the agents. The task consisted of listening to a few call-center transactions and writing down the problem or purpose of the calls. John works with the agents all at once, because they all listened to the same calls. First, they listen as a class to one call at a time. Then John leads a discussion with the group, making sure that each agent takes part and states an opinion. Then they work as a class to review the answers that the agents did for homework. John asks the coaches if they agree with the responses.

Preparation and presentation (30 minutes): After several sessions, John has received feedback from the coaches that the agents are not clarifying information and are often recording it incorrectly, so John has chosen an activity to practice clarification skills. First, he introduces the topic by asking the agents in one group and the coaches in another to discuss why they think errors are made in the call center. The groups then share their ideas. Several students report that they feel they should know the language and therefore should not need to ask for clarification.

John provides the agents with several opportunities to observe native speakers interacting on the phone and shows the agents how even native speakers often ask for clarification and summarize an interaction. John teaches them strategies for clarifying and prepares role-play cards for them. Then he asks the different agents to role-play with a coach to help them practice the interactions.

Personalized practice (45 minutes): John asks the coaches to review the notes they have accumulated during the week with the agent they trained. During this time, John meets with individual agents and their coaches so he can provide suggestions and positive feedback. John notices that one of the agents is having trouble with listening strategies. This agent tends to write the information without listening to the full message. John realizes the problem and gives some individual instruction. John is then prepared to give similar instruction to the class.

Extension (20 minutes): John uses several audio examples from the company's formalized trainings. He asks the agents to listen to the first passage without writing anything down. Then John asks them to repeat what they hear. After they have finished discussing the recording, John asks the agents to write down what they hear. John helps the agents relax by telling them that there is no pressure in the activity, and that it is more of a game to see how much they can remember.

Assessment (10 minutes): The agents are assessed regularly so they can see their own progress at the end of each session. John tailors the instruction, based on his perception of the agents' performance, their own perception of their work, and the coaches' observations. John establishes one objective for each session and continues to work with the agents and coaches until they are somewhat proficient.

Application (20 minutes): The agents periodically go into the mock call rooms, where a veteran call-center agent places a series of simulated calls to the agents with commentary during

2:3 Activities and Strategies	
2:4 Learner Considerations	
2:2 Instructor Role	
2:3 Activities and Strategies	
2:4 Learner Considerations	
2:3 Activities and Strategies	
2:4 Learner Considerations	
2:2 Instructor Role	
2:3 Activities and Strategies	
2:4 Learner Considerations	

and after each call. This becomes an application as well as an assessment to help the agents feel confident that they can do the work on their own. John also listens to these exchanges in order to provide specific feedback on the language aspects of the agents' performance during these calls and to identify future objectives.

Discussion

A. Study the vignette. List different ways in which John offers instruction to both the coaches and the agents.

[Answer Key A: Answers include 3-hour training to coaches, encourages open discussion between coaches and agents, provides feedback individually to both coaches and agents, conducts regular assessments to help both coaches and agents see how they are progressing.]

B. Discuss the following:

1. John uses question strategies to encourage students to think critically about what they are doing. Identify some of the questions in the vignette and think of other ways he could have encouraged critical thinking.

2. Instruction must include real-life applications. Students should not be asked to apply what they learn until they have all the tools they need. What preparation is given to ensure that the agents are ready to apply what they have learned outside of the classroom or in real-life situations?

C. Recall a lesson you have given or plan a new one. How do you encourage students to use the target language outside of the classroom? How can you ensure that they are ready to use the language successfully on their own?

Vignette: College/University

Standard 2: Instructing

Background

This vignette describes instruction in a three-unit ESL course at a public university in Florida. The instructor is one of several full-time teachers in the program, which serves both international students and immigrants. The 24 students in the class come from different countries in Asia, Central America, and Europe. In this prefreshman reading/writing course, students are introduced to the writing process with a focus on the essay's form and organization. They explore how to include supporting detail from personal experience and readings; to paraphrase, refer to, summarize, and cite readings; and to do in-class writing. The reading component includes critical reading and annotation, preparation of a reading/response journal, and techniques for peer reading and self-editing.

The instructor, Maria Alvarez, has taught the course several times and follows the program-determined curriculum goals, objectives, and required assignments: three out-of-class and two in-class essays. The class meets twice a week for 75 minutes and uses a popular ESL writing textbook that features readings and information about writing that somewhat parallels the course content. The first unit covers two writing heuristics (brainstorming, clustering), essay focus and overall organization, strategies for revision and peer reading, and recommendations for keeping a reading/response journal. The vignette describes a class session (4 weeks into the semester) that introduces the second unit and focuses on an expository essay the students will write on new technologies, a topic treated in three short readings (expository and personal essays) that the class has completed.

Vignette

Maria arrives 5 minutes before the start of class, sets up the overhead projector, and writes the agenda and the homework on the board.

Warm-up (7 minutes): After collecting the portfolios from the first unit and making some positive comments on their completion of the unit, Maria tells the students that their next reading/writing topic will be new technologies. She writes the topic on the board and asks the class to write down whatever comes to mind. (This thinking time helps everyone, but it allows the more reticent students to contribute "prepared participation.") Maria then writes students' ideas on the board as they volunteer them, using a cluster format and asking the students to take notes. After a couple of minutes, she asks them to spend 3 minutes speaking with a partner about anything that interests them from the cluster on the board or a related topic not on the board. Then she calls on several volunteers to say briefly what they discussed. (This elicits some points she has predicted and some she hasn't.)

Presentation 1 (5 minutes): Reminding the class that they just practiced the idea-generation strategies of brainstorming and clustering, she tells them that today they will learn and practice new strategies—freewriting and looping—to prepare them for the readings and to help them

| 2:1 Classroom Management |
| 2:2 Instructor Role |
| 2:3 Activities and Strategies |
| 2:4 Learner Considerations |

| 2:3 Activities and Strategies |

develop ideas for papers. She asks them to guess what freewriting means, elicits responses (apparently some of the students have done this before), and clarifies that it is continuous writing on a topic for a short period of time without stopping. She provides a bit more detail, and explains that they should not worry about form or content when freewriting. She then walks students through looping, which is a series of opportunities to reflect on the freewriting they have done and writing again using the previous ideas as starting points.

2:3 Activities and Strategies

Practice and follow-up (12 minutes): She then puts two general topics for freewriting on the board, both of which serve as schema building for the readings in the unit—"e-mail" and "technology in your life"—and asks students to choose one topic and freewrite for 8 minutes, pointing out that she will not collect their papers. This encourages students to be more candid in their writing. Maria does the freewriting as well, writing on a transparency. Because this is their first attempt at freewriting, she thinks it more important to model the technique than to monitor their writing; also, she knows that freewriting is not a preferred or easy strategy for many learners and that what they write may be highly personal. When the time is up, she asks students how it went (difficult, strange, interesting, etc.), puts her freewriting on the overhead projector, and reads it aloud, showing them that it is messy and disorganized and has some blank spots. She elicits quick responses to the content of her freewrite (agreement, disagreement, similar points, different points) and takes notes on the board.

2:2 Instructor Role

2:3 Activities and Strategies

Presentation 2 (3 minutes): To introduce the idea of looping, she asks students to select something in her writing that interests them or needs clarification or development. She marks their suggestion with a highlighter, then explains that looping means choosing a point in the writing (called a "hot spot") and then freewriting about it.

2:3 Activities and Strategies

Practice and follow-up 2 (25 minutes): She has the students choose and underline one idea in their writing that they would like to develop, and to freewrite on this for 8 minutes. As they read, mark, and then write, she does the same on a new transparency. She then reads her writing to the class, asks them to identify a new hot spot from it, and directs them to do the same with their most recent writing. Each time students write by reflecting on their previous work, it is considered a new loop. She follows up by asking students to describe their reactions to this process, noting comments on the board about how brainstorming or clustering can trigger ideas. She reminds them that prereading activities like this one increase background knowledge, schema activation (thinking about what they already know), and vocabulary familiarity, and she emphasizes the usefulness of freewriting and looping for generating and developing ideas for writing. She tells them to start their Unit 2 portfolio with these freewrites and says that they will freewrite again for a longer time period after discussing the readings they will complete during the unit. She concludes by giving them information on the unit essay assignment.

Presentation 3 and follow-up (10 minutes): Maria hands out a one-page description of the essay assignment that includes these sections: background, essay topic, purpose and audience, requirements (e.g., length, grading criteria), and due dates for three drafts. She reads the handout to them, checking comprehension as she goes. She then has the students work in groups of three with the textbook section entitled "Clarify an Assignment" to discuss the questions printed there. As the groups report back, she notes responses on the board so students can add information on the assignment sheet. She asks the class to compare this assignment to the one they just completed for Unit 1. She explains that they will review this assignment again before their first draft is due, but that they should have their essay task in mind as they discuss the readings and work more on writing techniques.

Wrap-up (5 minutes): Pointing to the lists on the board, Maria ends the class by reviewing what they have covered and giving the homework, allowing time for questions. She adds one final task: answering a question (that she writes on the board) in several sentences in their reading journals—"What interests you most about these readings and why?" She also asks them to e-mail this answer to three of their classmates and to print out the e-mails they receive (to put in their portfolios). She ends the class with encouragement about their preliminary work for this unit.

2:4 Learner Considerations

Discussion

A. Study the vignette. Below are the steps Maria takes to give her lesson. Number the steps to arrange them in the correct order.

_____ Instructor presents a new unit assignment.

_____ Instructor presents a topic.

_1_ Instructor writes the agenda on the board.

_____ Students brainstorm through listing ideas and clustering.

_____ Students freewrite.

_____ Students reflect by answering a question about the unit.

_____ Students write more by looping.

[Answer Key A: 6-2-1-3-4-7-5]

B. Discuss the following:

1. Maria's lesson includes some group work—students work in pairs and three's (with self-selected groups) and in groups of four (with teacher-selected groups). How do Maria's strategies meet instructional goals? What are the advantages and disadvantages of self-selected groups and of teacher-selected groups?

2. Maria regularly has students read each other's writing to give feedback on content; however, she does not do that in this lesson. Why might she avoid that approach in this case? Discuss whether you use peer reading in your class and under what circumstances. How does it promote reading/writing skills?

C. Identify and discuss features of the instruction that seem especially salient to you. Tell how they match the performance indicators for this standard, and how you might use or adapt them in your classes.

Vignette: Intensive English

Standard 2: Instructing

Background

This vignette describes a low-intermediate ESL class taught as part of an intensive English program (IEP) housed in a small liberal arts college in North Carolina. The instructor is one of two full-time teachers in the program, which serves a total of 40 international students. The students come from different countries in South America, the Middle East, and Asia. All are on student visas and studying in the United States on a full-time basis (approximately 25 hours per week). About half of the students plan to transfer to other colleges or universities in the United States and enroll in degree programs. The others have come to the United States solely to study English, and plan to return to their countries in order to resume their professional and educational activities.

The ESL class has 16 students. It follows a content-based approach and explores global topics, which encourage students to think critically about current issues. The course focuses on providing students with oral and written skills needed for successful communication in academic, professional, and social situations. This particular lesson, based on a video-viewing activity, is part of a unit on the environment. The video explores the topic of animal habitats. The lesson is based on a well-organized lesson plan with four steps: preview, presentation, exploration, and assessment. It also sets the stage for an extension activity, which will be introduced in the next class.

Vignette

Rick Gomez, the teacher, has spent the last few days preparing supporting materials for a video about animal habitats, an excellent resource for the unit his class is studying on the environment. However, because this is an authentic video produced by National Geographic, Rick knows that his intermediate-level students will need considerable scaffolding in order to make sense of the content. He has to plan the activities carefully.

2:1 Classroom Management

Previously, Rick watched the video several times, taking notes on the particular details he wanted his students to learn. The video is 20 minutes long and includes short segments about nine different animal habitats in the world. Rick offers flashcards that introduce important vocabulary and activate students' background knowledge before viewing the video. Then he organizes the viewing as a jigsaw activity. To model the procedure Rick wants each group to follow, he explains that the class as a whole will watch the first segment about polar regions and complete a handout with comprehension questions and short reading passages about the habitat. Then, Rick will divide the class into eight pairs, each responsible for a different habitat. The pairs will take turns watching their video segments while noting important information to share later with the other groups. Each group will complete the relevant postviewing questions and readings on their handout.

Rick arrives early in order to check the equipment and sort out the materials he will need for the class. He plays a short segment of his video in order to adjust the volume and check the image quality. He then lays out on his desk the materials he will need: copies of the handout and two sets of flashcards, one set with animal names and another set with corresponding pictures. Rick has 16 students in the class, so he has eight flashcards in each set.

Preview (20 minutes): As students enter the classroom, Rick hands out a flashcard to each person. He instructs students to sit down and not show their flashcards to others. When everyone has arrived, he begins a find-your-partner activity. A student who has a flashcard with an animal name must find someone who has the picture of that same animal. After students find their partners, Rick instructs the pairs to sit together and brainstorm ideas on the places where their animals live, the food they eat, and so on. The pairs then share their ideas with the class. During this discussion, Rick elicits vocabulary and discusses important concepts related to the content of the video. Rick tells the students to stay seated where they are because they will continue to work with the same partners during the video activity.

2:2 Instructor Role

2:3 Activities and Strategies

Presentation (30 minutes): Rick mutes the TV volume, and the class watches the introductory segment of the video in which the term *habitat* is defined. Based only on the scenes they see, the class makes predictions about the content of the video. Rick writes down all their ideas on the blackboard. Then, Rick turns on the volume and rewinds the video to the beginning. The class watches and listens to the same segment. They check their predictions written on the blackboard and discuss the definition of *habitat*. Now the class is ready to watch the rest of the video, in which information about different habitats is presented.

2:2 Instructor Role

2:3 Activities and Strategies

Exploration (45 minutes): The handout Rick prepared includes nine identical worksheets with a map of the world so students can color in the location of the habitat, and with space for them to write down characteristics of the habitat and to list the animals that live there. The handout also includes short readings with comprehension questions about each habitat. Rick decided to work through the first habitat region with the class as a whole in order to model the activity for the students before the jigsaw task. The class watches the segment about polar regions and completes the first worksheet as a group. After discussing the answers, Rick gives the class a list of the eight remaining habitats, and each pair chooses one habitat to work on. The jigsaw activity begins. Each "expert" pair takes turns going to the TV to watch the video segment about their chosen habitat and then completes the worksheet. The other pairs work on the reading section about the habitat they have been assigned while awaiting their turn to watch the video. After all the pairs have watched their video segment and filled out the information on their worksheet, Rick regroups the students into two big groups of eight students, each consisting of one member from each pair. In the big groups, each participant shares the content about his or her assigned habitat. Group members listen to the information shared by each "expert" and fill in their worksheets. Rick visits each group so he can check the accuracy of the information that is being shared.

2:1 Classroom Management

2:2 Instructor Role

2:3 Activities and Strategies

Assessment (10 minutes): Rick is constantly monitoring students' learning through observation and completion of activities. He helps groups by answering questions and clarifying tasks when necessary. After the jigsaw activity, he shows a map of the world on a transparency and asks students to help him color in the regions of the nine different habitats. He takes this opportunity to ask the class specific questions about each region.

2:1 Classroom Management

2:3 Activities and Strategies

2:4 Learner Considerations

Extension (10 minutes): Before ending class, Rick announces to students that they will be working on a video project during the next two classes. Each expert pair will be producing a short nature video about their habitat, discussing threats to animals and plants in the region. For homework, he asks students to review the information on their worksheets (from both the video and the readings) and to highlight important details to be included in the video they will produce.

Next class: The next day, Rick gives a test covering all nine habitats, and he allows students to refer to their worksheets in order to answer the questions.

Discussion

A. Study the vignette. Rick explores academic content in this intermediate-level class. To make content accessible to his students, he uses a variety of resources. List the resources he uses.

[Answer Key A: Answers include flashcards, video, worksheets]

B. Discuss the following:

1. Rick uses different grouping strategies to meet his instructional goals. Discuss the cooperative learning techniques (e.g., pair work, jigsaw) incorporated in the lesson. Would these techniques work in your own classroom? Why or why not?

2. Rick assesses his students' learning through observation and their completion of activities. What other assessment measures would you use for this lesson?

C. Make a list of activities from this lesson you would like to incorporate into your own lesson. Explain how you might approach it.

Vignette: English as a Foreign Language

Standard 2: Instructing

Background

This vignette describes a beginning English as a foreign language (EFL) class taught at a center in Medellin, Colombia. The instructor, Luis Restrepo, has been a full-time teacher at the center for more than 15 years. He has a bachelor's degree in English from a Colombian university and a master's degree in teaching English to speakers of other languages (TESOL) from a U.S. university. Luis is one of 30 teachers at the center. The center serves approximately 800 students, most of whom are working individuals, college students, or homemakers who want to learn English for business, travel, or academic purposes. Luis teaches eight different classes, a total of 24 hours per week.

Luis and his colleagues follow a curriculum set by the center's academic department. The mandated textbooks follow a theme-based approach and integrate instruction of the four language skills with an emphasis on oral communication. Typical courses run 3 hours per week for one semester. The curriculum consists of 12 levels of instruction. Students are placed in levels according to the results of a placement test that they take when first enrolling in the program.

Luis is preparing to teach a class of beginners that meets on Tuesday and Thursday mornings. All 18 students are young adults who attend the class before going to work in the morning.

Vignette

Luis arrives in the classroom 10 minutes early to set up his materials. He writes an agenda on the board and makes sure he has everything he will need to conduct the class. As the students enter the room, they chat about the weekend. After everyone arrives, Luis begins the lesson.

2:1 Classroom Management

Preview (15 minutes): Luis puts the students into groups of three or four. He passes out a handout with pictures of several types of food and a chart with six columns for the following categories: (1) breads and cereals group, (2) vegetable group, (3) fruit group, (4) meat group, (5) dairy group, and (6) fats, oils, and sweets. He tells the students to first to label each picture and then to write the item in the correct column. The groups work fast. Most of this work is review for them, but a few of the words are new. Luis moves around the room, checking the students' work and answering questions. After they finish categorizing all the food items, Luis debriefs the activity by categorizing the words on the blackboard and engaging the class in dialogue. He asks questions such as, "Do you like steak?" "Do you know how to bake a cake?" "What is your favorite seafood restaurant?" "What do you usually eat for breakfast?" The students enjoy talking about their eating habits and sharing their likes and dislikes. They even offer restaurant recommendations.

2:2 Instructor Role
2:3 Activities and Strategies
2:4 Learner Considerations

Presentation (15 minutes): Luis tells the class that he will play the tape of a dialogue between two people. He asks the class to listen carefully and try to answer two questions: "Where are they?" and "What are they doing?" He plays the conversation and asks the students to share their ideas. He asks the students to support their answers with information from the dialogue.

2:2 Instructor Role
2:3 Activities and Strategies

For example, a student says, "I think they are in the supermarket because they are talking about chicken." Another student says, "I think it is a restaurant because they asked for the menu."

Luis then asks the students to open their textbooks and look at the picture that illustrates the dialogue. Seeing the picture of a couple ordering food at a restaurant allows the students to confirm or disconfirm their predictions. Then, Luis has the students listen to the recording again and complete the textbook activity, which asks them to list the foods and drinks ordered by each person. Luis asks students to compare their answers in the book with a partner, and he circulates to confirm that students have listed the correct written responses.

2:1 Classroom Management
2:2 Instructor Role

Practice (15 minutes): Luis divides the students into groups of three or four and explains that they will role-play a restaurant scenario. One person will be the server and the others will be customers. He has several menus from different types of restaurants and asks the groups to choose a restaurant for their role-play. After each group selects a menu, Luis models the activity with two students. He asks the students to sit at his table at the center of the classroom. He plays the role of the server and initiates a short conversation. After completing the model, he asks the groups to compose and practice their own dialogues.

While the students are composing their dialogues, Luis moves around the room and offers help when needed. The groups then practice their dialogues, after which Luis asks three groups to perform their role-play for the class.

Extension: Before ending the class, Luis assigns a short task for homework. He asks the students to write a set of instructions on how to prepare a simple food (such as rice or grilled meat) or drink (such as coffee or tea).

2:1 Classroom Management
2:2 Instructor Role

After the students leave, Luis spends a few minutes reviewing his lesson plan. He had planned to start showing a short video of a cooking show but did not have time. He decides, instead, to show the video at the beginning of the next class, before reviewing the students' homework. Working in groups, the students will then create their own cooking shows, which Luis will videotape. Luis estimates that he will need at least two more sessions to complete these activities.

Discussion

A. Study the vignette. Identify the different techniques Luis uses to

   1. verify comprehension

   2. facilitate discussion

   [Answer Key A: Verify comprehension: Answers may include classifying activities, questioning, and circulating through the class. Facilitate discussion: Answers may include questioning strategies and predicting activities.]

B. Discuss the following:

   1. How does Luis foster his students' reasoning, problem-solving, and critical-thinking skills? Discuss at least two strategies.

   2. Luis works hard to promote constructive interactions among his students. Make a list of new things he could do to accomplish this goal.

C. Would you implement some of the same techniques as Luis in your class? Which ones? Why or why not?

Standard 3
Assessing

Standard 3: Assessing

Standard 3
Assessing

Teachers recognize the importance of and are able to gather and interpret information about learning and performance to promote the continuous intellectual and linguistic development of each learner. Teachers use knowledge of student performance to make decisions about planning and instruction "on the spot" and for the future. Teachers involve learners in determining what will be assessed and provide constructive feedback to learners, based on assessments of their learning.

Teachers understand the interdependent relationship between teaching and assessment, and the characteristics, uses, advantages, and limitations of different types of assessments. Therefore teachers select, use, design, or modify assessments appropriate to learning objectives, the learner, and the learning context. Teachers use a variety of formal and informal assessment tools, which may include class work, portfolios, in-class tasks, student self-assessments, peer assessments, instructor-generated tests, and standardized tests. Assessment tools should allow teachers to enhance learners' knowledge, evaluate individual learner and class progress toward predetermined objectives, and modify their instruction as needed; ideally, they should allow learners to apply acquired knowledge and skills in realistic contexts. Teachers should evaluate the cultural sensitivity of assessment tools in order to reduce bias; involve learners in naming signs of progress and evaluating that performance; maintain records of learner performance; and communicate assessment results knowledgably and responsibly both to learners and to current and future schools and employers.

Standard 3: Assessing Performance Indicators

3:1 Need for Assessment

- demonstrates a recognition of the importance of obtaining information about learner performance
- ties assessment to learning objectives

3:2 Types of Assessment

- uses a variety of formal and informal assessment tools appropriate for the context and desired results
- uses assessment that is multimodal, systematic, and purposeful
- uses assessment tools that allow learners to demonstrate their learning
- uses assessment tools that are culturally sensitive, appropriate, and equitable
- uses assessment tools that are instructor generated and standardized

3:3 Evaluation of Results

- gathers and interprets information about learner background, preferences, expectations, and goals
- monitors learning as it happens in the classroom
- gathers, interprets, and documents information about performance before, during, and after instruction

3:4 Learner Considerations

- engages learners in self-assessment and monitoring of their progress
- uses learner feedback on instructional methods and approaches in the design of appropriate assessments
- provides constructive feedback to learners based on assessments of their learning

3:5 Development and Changes

- evaluates the reliability and validity of instructor-generated and standardized assessment instruments
- uses assessment results and learner feedback to adjust or modify the future learning objectives

Vignette: Adult/Community

Standard 3: Assessing

Background

This vignette describes the assessment practices of an instructor in a small adult education program in New Mexico. The instructor considers it his responsibility to create an environment where students are anxious to advance and are working toward real and attainable goals. After exploring various techniques for determining student needs, progress, and overall preparedness for advancement, he found that assessment is the most effective tool to evaluate student progress, to validate his instructional methods, to modify or enhance future instruction, and, especially in the case of students who are uncomfortable about advancing because they feel they are not ready, to help students witness their personal progress and articulate their goals. The teacher in this vignette is a full-time instructor who communicates regularly with other instructors and shares ideas and successes as well as concerns. The class consists of 22 students from South America who are at a high-beginning level.

Vignette

Placement test: Ross Hinemann works at a school that administers a preliminary placement test that was created by the institution and is reviewed and modified regularly for reliability and validity. Despite the purported reliability of the test, Ross is continually faced with students of varied ability and language proficiency. He realizes that the complex nature of language learning makes it extremely difficult to measure proficiency. Therefore, he is a supporter of multiple measures to evaluate his students once they arrive in his classroom. After consulting the placement score and administering a preliminary classroom evaluation, he immediately reports any obvious misplacement to the English as a second language (ESL) coordinator so the students in question can be retested or enrolled in the appropriate class.

> 3:2 Types of Assessment
>
> 3:5 Development and Changes

First-week assessments: Ross is animated, and his students are engaged. Ross attributes his success to his understanding of student needs. After 3 weeks, he knows students by name and understands many of their goals and challenges. On the first day of class, he administers a student survey in which he asks the students questions in order to learn information that might influence his approach. He realizes that students learn English best when the course topics interest them or seem necessary to survival in the United States.

> 3:3 Evaluation of Results
>
> 3:4 Learner Considerations

He also administers a standardized pretest on the first day, on which the first 10 questions test listening, the next 10 assess reading, and the final 10 target grammar. He processes the results immediately in order to review them with each student during the following class period. During the second class period, Ross puts a writing prompt on the board and asks students to write a paragraph, explaining that he will collect all work after 20 minutes and that students should not worry if they cannot complete the task in the allotted time. During the 20 minutes, Ross speaks with each student individually about his or her pretest from the previous day. He encourages students and, based on his preliminary findings, suggests an area of focus for the

> 3:2 Types of Assessment
>
> 3:3 Evaluation of Results

course. He reads student writing without correcting it and saves it for portfolios that students will maintain throughout the semester.

Ross has determined that the class is at a slightly higher level than the last group he taught, and the students are largely interested in getting jobs or better jobs. Based on this information, he decides to modify his lesson plans and to push the group more than he had anticipated.

3:2 Types of Assessment

3:3 Evaluation of Results

3:5 Development and Changes

Informal classroom observation: Ross's lessons are task based, and the students are actively engaged and rarely sit quietly during class. Ross tries to elicit as much as possible from students rather than merely presenting information. He rarely sits at the teacher's desk and is always aware of the lesson objective. He carefully observes the students, listening to their responses and monitoring the tasks they must complete. In today's lesson, for example, the objective is to describe people. Ross teaches about height, hair color, and eye color, explaining the use of *to be* to describe height (*He is tall.*) and *have* to describe hair and eye color (*She has blond hair.*). Students have trouble using the verbs correctly, so Ross decides to present the information differently after students have practiced it and to offer them a second opportunity to drill with these structures.

3:2 Types of Assessment

3:4 Learner Considerations

Every week, Ross gives his students a spelling test based on the vocabulary in the unit. Students exchange papers afterward, and peers correct them. Ross knows that the test does not measure proficiency, and that students with little or no formal education will have trouble with these assessments. In Ross's program, instructors do not issue grades, so he does not maintain a grade book. Instead, he has students maintain weekly test results in a chart because he believes that doing so encourages them to establish goals and improve skills.

Unit assessments: At the end of every unit (about every 2 weeks), Ross passes out a blank 3 × 5 card to each student so they can assess the class. He writes three or four questions about the class on the board. He encourages students to be honest because these cards can help make him a better teacher. He tells them to write the answers to the questions and not to write their names on the cards. After the health unit, he asks "What activities did you like the best?" and offers the following possible responses: group work about good nutrition, writing a paragraph about your health, the health survey, or class presentations. Ross asks a student to collect the cards and then tallies and discusses the results with the class.

3:1 Need for Assessment

3:5 Development and Changes

3:4 Learner Considerations

Ross also gives a unit exam to assess student learning. He uses a test from the book that targets objectives from the unit. After each use, he identifies questions that most students miss, evaluates if the problems result from his shortcomings or poorly framed questions, notes ways in which he might improve his instruction, and modifies the test accordingly.

Finally, Ross asks students to evaluate their own learning at the end of a unit. He restates the objectives of the lessons from the unit and has students check the topics they have mastered on an objectives checklist.

Ross also makes use of personal portfolios. He does not have file space in his classroom so he asks students to maintain their own. He collects them every 4 weeks to evaluate student progress. The portfolio consists of the student's needs survey, the 20-minute writing samples he has them do every 4 weeks, the spelling test progress chart, the objectives checklist, and various activities or projects that students are asked to include. Each time he collects the portfolios, students assess their progress from the beginning of class and report on a 3 × 5 card if they have not progressed, have progressed a little, or have progressed considerably. Ross collects these cards and evaluates student perceptions of the class. Then during a 20-minute writing task, he speaks to each student to discuss their progress. In this case, Ross finds a student who reports that she is not progressing. He discusses her portfolio with her in detail, identifying areas of improvement in her writing so she can see concrete evidence of progress. Ross meets with another student who has not improved and suggests additional homework and changes to study habits.

3:2 Types of Assessment

3:4 Learner Considerations

End-of-term assessment: During the last week of the semester, Ross reviews the portfolios with the students. He makes some recommendations, and the class goes over the checklist of objectives as a group. After they review areas that many students are finding difficult, he administers the posttest, which is another form of the pretest. He tabulates the results quickly but carefully. On the final day, Ross assigns a meaningful task and meets with each student individually to make a recommendation about whether the student should advance based on his informal observations, the portfolio, the student's confidence level, and the results of the pretest and posttest.

3:2 Types of Assessment

3:4 Learner Considerations

Discussion

A. Ross uses multiple measures to identify student progress. Rank the different types of assessments that Ross uses from what you consider most effective (1) to least effective (10).

____ Placement Test

____ Student Survey (needs assessment)

____ Portfolios

____ 20-Minute Write

____ Informal Observation

____ Spelling Tests

____ Unit Tests

____ 3 × 5 Card Assessment

____ Student Personal Assessment

____ Posttest

[Answer Key A: Answers will vary.]

B. Discuss the following:

1. Discuss the ranking you did in Exercise A above. Which type of assessment do you consider the most effective and why? Which tool do you think was most effective for Ross and why?

2. What did Ross do with the information he received from the following assessments?

Placement Test _____

Study Survey (needs assessment) _____

Portfolios _____

20-Minute Write _____

Informal Observation _____

Spelling Tests _____

Unit Tests _____

3 × 5 Card Assessment _____

Student Personal Assessment _____

Posttest _____

C. Make a list of additional or other assessments that you might try in your class.

Vignette: Workplace

Standard 3: Assessing

Background

This vignette describes a workplace program that was established in order to improve the performance and communication of workers in a packaging plant in Nebraska. The management of the rather large company recognized the potential of employees who had worked at the plant for several years but had never been promoted principally because of limited English language skills. Also there was a great deal of turnover in the assembly and other entry-level areas, partially because employees did not view their jobs as a stepping-stone to better employment within the company.

The company subsequently hired an outside agency to work directly with the employees. By observing the company environment and listening to verbal exchanges, consultants determined that employees needed to expand their English vocabulary, learn to circumlocute, produce more comprehensible speech, attain greater grammatical correctness, and improve pronunciation in order to work in a variety of positions within the company. The information they gathered enabled the outside company to establish objectives, curricula, and assessment tools targeting numeracy, task skills, and safety issues.

The company has well over 400 employees, of whom 100 would benefit from English instruction. Despite the efforts of middle managers to demonstrate that the benefits of the program outweigh the costs, upper level managers continue to question the value of the instruction and have not yet decided to expand the program. Consequently, only employees who wish to participate in the program, and have the potential for advancement, can do so.

Vignette

Needs survey: Joanne Freedman's charge, as an instructor in the workplace setting described above, is to develop and implement training using authentic situations in familiar settings. To do this, she has to learn about the industry and get to know the employees through needs assessments and surveys. Much of the other preliminary work has been done for her, because she has been given a curriculum and corpus of vocabulary. Even with these tools, Joanne knows that every class is different and every employee has particular needs and learning styles. Therefore Joanne, who has been teaching in this setting for more than a year, always starts a new class with a needs survey. This tool includes questions about the employee's background and his or her personal work goals at the company and beyond. Joanne studies the results of the survey so she can customize instruction in order to meet student needs. The information she gathers helps her to motivate students and provides a connection between the work environment and the language the employees are learning.

| 3:1 Need for Assessment |
| 3:3 Evaluation of Results |

After administering the needs survey, Joanne sees that most of her 20 students do not have long-term goals in the company; however, she also learns that they do not know what potential opportunities are available to them. Therefore, she plans to provide students with many opportunities to learn about positions other than those of their immediate supervisors in quality control, purchasing, and customer service. She enlists the help of employees in each of these areas to enhance instruction and to add to the authenticity of the course.

3:1 Need for Assessment

3:2 Types of Assessment

3:3 Evaluation of Results

Pre-assessment: Joanne also gives a pretest that she created based on predetermined norms on the first day of class. The test, based on standardized tests for the industry that have been gauged to be valid and reliable, helps Joanne to assess the employees' progress and how well they could function in different positions. Although the results indicate that the students' skill levels are extremely diverse, Joanne cannot separate the group because she is the only instructor and the company has only authorized one class. In order to find ways to reach each student using multilevel strategies, she studies the curriculum, reviews her notes about the students, determines where each one falls on the yardsticks that have been established for the employees, and identifies the objectives she should cover during the 24 weeks of the course.

Ongoing assessment: Joanne starts a portfolio process with her students. The portfolio includes a list of yardsticks with performance objectives, test scores, and work samples. The objectives appear as a list that the student checks off and the instructor approves when an employee has demonstrated a particular skill. By offering this ongoing assessment of student progress, the portfolio motivates the students. Meanwhile, the portfolio demonstrates the program's success and provides concrete data to the administration when employees are being considered for advancement.

3:2 Types of Assessment

3:3 Evaluation of Results

3:4 Learner Considerations

3:5 Development and Changes

Among other activities, Joanne relies on role-plays in her instruction. Twice a week, she videotapes the role-plays. The students view the tapes at subsequent meetings and critique their peers and themselves with a very simple rubric established by the instructor. The process of self-evaluation helps students see their progress and feel motivated to advance further, so Joanne often replays recordings from previous weeks to show students how they have improved. Joanne also uses these recordings to modify instruction. For example, as Joanne reflects on student performance in the videos, she notices that nearly all the students mispronounce final consonants, and that these errors are impeding comprehension. She decides to develop a series of activities that will provide an opportunity for students to listen and judge meaning. She takes these examples from a series of recordings from the plant where the students work that were produced when the curriculum was established by her agency. They include examples of situations where the final consonant sound affects meaning. She creates a series of multiple-choice questions based on the recordings and asks students to identify the meaning.

3:3 Evaluation of Results

Accountability and assessment: In a workplace setting, companies pay a substantial amount of money to provide their employees with English instruction; they pay the agency providing the service, provide employee release time, and may offer additional salary to employees who attend classes. In this case, the company sees the benefit of such an arrangement because management believes it will improve morale, reduce the turnover rate, and motivate longtime employees to qualify for advancement. In order to justify the cost, however, the management hires two independent assessors to evaluate recorded interviews twice during the 24-week course, on weeks 6 and 18, to assess student performance based on a standardized rubric. At the end of the course, the students take a standardized test so the administration can track their progress as a justification for continuing the program.

Discussion

A. Study the vignette. List the types of assessments that Joanne uses in the course.

[Answer Key A: Answers include needs assessments and surveys, pretests, portfolios, and student oral performance evaluations.]

B. Discuss the following:

1. What aspect of the assessment process described in the vignette would be most problematic or difficult?

2. What is the purpose of each type of assessment described in the vignette?

C. What other assessments could be incorporated into this project? Explain how the same assessments could be used in other workplace settings. Compare these to assessments you have used in a workplace setting.

Vignette: College/University

Standard 3: Assessing

Background

This vignette describes the assessment practices of an instructor in a 16-week, credit-bearing grammar-for-writing course in an ESL program at a large urban public university in northern California. The university offers multiple sections of all four levels of courses in the ESL program, in order to prepare students for and support them in their academic work. The grammar-for-writing course focuses on developing grammatical accuracy and editing skills. The students in the program are mostly freshmen, sophomores, and community college transfers from Asian countries, a mix of international students, recent immigrants, and long-term residents. Many of the immigrant students hold part- or full-time jobs, and most members of this class are concurrently enrolled in an ESL writing course and their academic content classes.

The part-time lecturer, Melissa Allen, has taught in this program for 10 years, teaching three or four different courses each semester. She meets regularly with other instructors in the program so that they can standardize instructional goals, materials, and assessment procedures for the individual courses. Melissa sees herself as a contributor to and implementer of the program-wide assessment measures, which are designed to ensure that students are placed in the appropriate classes, are meeting instructional goals, are prepared to advance to the next level, and are given support in and beyond the classroom for their individual English needs.

Vignette

3:1 Need for Assessment

3:2 Types of Assessment

3:5 Development and Changes

Placement test: At the beginning of each semester, the program administers a placement test that was developed in house, is revised regularly, and consists of (1) a discourse-level grammar editing task and (2) an expository reading designed to elicit two writing samples: a summary and an expository essay. Students are placed in one of the four levels of a particular class on the basis of their performance on these assessments. The grammar-editing task is especially useful in placing students in the grammar-for-writing class. Melissa participates in the holistic scoring of the writing samples and assists in the placement of students.

3:1 Need for Assessment

3:2 Types of Assessment

3:3 Evaluation of Results

First-week assessments: Melissa knows that students are quite accurately placed in her class, but she uses several initial diagnostic measures to learn more about her students, who always have diverse ethnic backgrounds, varying degrees of academic sophistication, and a wide range of grammar, editing, and writing ability. She asks each student (usually 25 in the class) to complete a handout with information including visa status, ethnicity and language background, academic level and major, prior experience in ESL courses, and work schedule. This gives her some information about the students to help her target instruction and to group students appropriately. Melissa relies heavily on group work in the class and often pairs international students who possess strong grammar knowledge but weak oral skills with longtime residents who have strong oral skills but weak grammar knowledge. The initial handout also informs her about how acculturated her students are, and whether to avoid certain discussions, such as those that rely on comparisons between students' native countries and the United States.

Because Melissa feels strongly that assessment should mirror her instruction, which integrates reading, writing, and grammar at the discourse level, she has assigned in-class writing on a prompt related to a reading that the class has read and discussed. She also believes that assessments should be "biased for the best" (in this case, stronger students must have something to say and weaker readers should not be penalized for lack of comprehension or ideas about the reading). She requires that students spend at least 20 minutes in class editing their papers, because one of her course goals is that students learn how to edit their work and she needs to see what students can already do. This writing sample, along with another more objective measure (a paragraph-level editing task), allows her to see the students' individual strengths and problem areas in order to focus the course content and identify students who may need extra help from her or the campus learning center.

3:3 Evaluation of Results
3:5 Development and Changes

Students use their performance on these tasks for the next assessment phase: self-assessment and goal-setting. Using Melissa's selective feedback and their own analysis of their writing samples, the students formulate prioritized grammar and writing goals for the first half of the course. She facilitates this process by leading a whole-class discussion in which students brainstorm grammar and writing skills they want to improve, note particular areas they need to work on, and then brainstorm in groups ways to improve their skills and check their progress. Because she realizes that self-assessment and goal-setting may be unfamiliar, she explains the importance of personal goal-setting and the developmental nature of language learning. She believes that students who know what they want from a course become more directly engaged and responsible for their own learning.

Unit assessments: Each unit of the course lasts about 3 weeks and is built around a reading, the drafting and revision of a thematically related composition, and a focus on selected grammar points. Melissa informally assesses students' performance on a number of class activities during each unit (answers to comprehension and discussion questions about the reading; freewrites, clusters, and composition drafts; group work on textual analysis, grammar, editing; and listening comprehension activities). She also regularly asks students, individually or in groups, to put work on the board for class discussion so the whole class can make corrections and suggestions. She sees herself as a collaborator in these informal assessments, helping the students monitor their progress as they address the goals they set and identify new goals.

3:2 Types of Assessment
3:4 Learner Considerations

At the end of the unit, she conducts an in-class editing workshop for peer-assessment. Students work in pairs or groups on papers that they have revised for content and edited for grammar based on the textbook editing guides and other reference materials, and then they put examples from their work on the board and discuss as a class. This self- and peer-assessment helps students to develop strategies for interacting with their own and others' writing, and to develop techniques for their own editing work. Melissa feels strongly that this structured and student-generated, question-driven peer assessment leads to greater success and learning than the more traditional approach of merely searching for errors.

When the students turn in their final papers (or when they prepare for a conference on a draft), Melissa has them attach a self-assessment cover sheet on which they respond to various prompts about the paper (e.g., what they liked, what they did well, what was difficult, what part of the paper they would like to improve). These reactions provide more context for her assessment of their papers and allow her to address individual concerns. When evaluating student

3:4 Learner Considerations
3:5 Development and Changes

papers, Melissa's feedback goal is clarity and guidance for future writing. She does minimal marking of errors, focusing on a few salient problems including those covered in the unit, such as verb tense, reported speech, and the use of punctuation that the students know. She writes an end comment on the content, focusing on the student's progress, and she uses a multitrait grading rubric that includes plus, check, and minus symbols of various components for content, grammar, and mechanics to match the tasks of the writing prompt. Melissa has found that such a rubric simplifies her assessment and grading procedure and helps her avoid excessive comments and questions that her students may not be able to process. Her students do further work with their returned papers—writing out corrections for selected errors, keeping a log of strengths and weaknesses (in both grammar and writing), and setting new goals based on her feedback. For further individualized work on grammar, she assigns downloadable exercises from the textbook Web site that she or a tutor can review with the student.

3:4 Learner Considerations
3:5 Development and Changes

Midterm and end-of-term assessment: At the end of the second, fourth, and final units, Melissa gives a test that includes a brief objective component (editing selected errors in a paragraph, completing a cloze activity, doing a dictation, etc.) and an in-class writing task (on a topic covered in the prior units) that she collects and returns at the next class for editing (30 minutes). Her feedback procedure on this writing is the same as for out-of-class writing, and leads to student follow-up work. At midterm and again at the end of the term, Melissa also asks students to fill out a self-assessment form on which they grade themselves, provide evaluative information about their performance on various course components, and list their strengths, achievements, and future goals. This self-assessment encourages students to feel responsible for and realistic about their performance, and it helps her identify problems and plan individualized assistance. At the end of the course, she assigns students a grade based on course components and their relative percentage (as specified at the beginning of the semester) and gives each student a paper showing the grade, how she arrived at that grade, and her recommendation for future English courses. When a student's final in-class and out-of-class papers hover between a pass and fail, Melissa has his or her writing evaluated by a team of other teachers of the same course, thus providing a check on her own grading reliability.

Discussion

A. List the different assessments that are discussed in this vignette.

Institution: _____

Teacher: _____

Student (self): _____

Peer: _____

[Answer Key A: Institution: placement test; Teacher: information sheet, writing sample, objective measures (pre-, mid-, and end-of-year), informal assessment, student writing; Student: self-assessments, goal setting, self-evaluation of performance; Peer: peer editing]

B. Discuss the following:

1. Summarize Melissa's beliefs about assessment. Where her beliefs are not stated, what might be her rationale for using or not using particular types? (Refer to the performance indicators for this standard for ideas.)

2. Identify and discuss

   a. the types of feedback Melissa gives on compositions (that are written in and out of class)

   b. the uses the students make of this feedback. What advantages do these procedures have for Melissa and for her students?

C. Discuss the various assessments that Melissa uses, compare her ideas about assessment to your own, and explain what motivated you to use forms of assessment that she implemented, or how you would use or change them in your class.

Vignette: Intensive English

Standard 3: Assessing

Background

This vignette describes the assessment practices of an instructor in a private intensive English program (IEP) located in an office building in downtown Denver, Colorado. The program uses assessment as a tool to enhance student learning, so instructors are encouraged to incorporate a variety of formal and informal assessment techniques into their daily class activities. Most of the students in this program plan to enter degree programs at U.S. colleges and universities and must therefore obtain a passing score on the Test of English as a Foreign Language (TOEFL). The program recognizes the need to prepare students for the TOEFL, as well as to expose them to other types of assessment they will likely encounter in their future college courses. The program offers four levels of instruction (beginning, low intermediate, high intermediate, and advanced); each course lasts approximately 10 weeks.

Sunida Bauer has been a part-time instructor in this school for the last 11 years. All 15 instructors in the program meet at the beginning and end of each term in order to discuss student placement and advancement to the next level. In addition, instructors teaching courses at the same level meet regularly to discuss student- and curriculum-related issues. Sunida teaches a high-intermediate reading/writing class, along with a team of three other instructors at the same level. The class described in this vignette has 16 students.

Vignette

3:1 Need for Assessment

3:2 Types of Assessment

3:4 Learner Considerations

Placement tests: At the beginning of each term, the school administers a placement test to all students who are entering the program. The test consists of three parts: an oral interview, a writing sample, and a commercially produced multiple-choice placement test that targets reading and listening comprehension. The program has been using this test for 4 years because it works well to differentiate students into four ability levels. The instructors produced the oral interview and the writing-sample materials in house. The oral interview employs pictures and role-play cards designed to elicit language at progressively higher levels of proficiency. The writing sample prompts students to write for 30 minutes on a topic of current interest. Two instructors grade both the oral interview and the writing sample holistically, using a scoring guide with descriptors for each level. To ensure that they are evaluating students consistently, instructors meet twice a year to recalibrate themselves as test scorers.

The program coordinator makes all decisions for level placement based on the results of the placement tests. However, instructors recognize that the performance of students who have just arrived in the country or who suffer from test anxiety, for example, may not reflect their actual abilities. Instructors routinely conduct diagnostic testing and observe students carefully during the first week of the term to check and correct any incorrect placement. Most students are placed in the same level for all courses. However, students whose scores show great variation between oral and written skills may be placed at a higher listening/speaking level and a lower reading/writing level, or vice versa.

Diagnostic testing and observation: Sunida's approach to teaching relies heavily on cooperative group activities. For this reason, she knows that it is important to foster an atmosphere of collaboration and trust from the outset. She wants her students to know each other and work well together, so she strives to build a sense of community in the classroom. She uses a getting-to-know-each-other activity that requires students to interview a partner and take notes during the conversation about family and academic backgrounds, likes and dislikes, and plans for the future. When students have finished interviewing a classmate, she asks everyone to introduce his or her partner orally to the class. Then, she has the students write a short essay about their partners. This activity serves two purposes: It gives both Sunida and the rest of the class the opportunity to learn personal information about all class members, and it provides Sunida with a sample of her students' writing that she can use for diagnostic purposes.

3:2 Types of Assessment
3:3 Evaluation of Results

On the following day, Sunida introduces the topic of the first unit of study: the U.S. family. Using information from the essays written on the first day, she engages the class in a discussion of their families. Then, she gives the students a short reading passage on this topic with comprehension questions. After all the students have completed the questions individually, she collects their answers and discusses the reading with the class.

The third day, after reviewing both the writing samples and the comprehension exercises, Sunida notices that one of the students seems to have much stronger reading and writing skills than the other students. She asks the program coordinator to look at the results of this student's placement test and discovers that his scores had placed him midway between the high-intermediate and advanced levels. She then shows the student's essay to the instructor who teaches the advanced reading/writing class, and he agrees that the student belongs in the advanced class. After discussing this option with Sunida, the student agrees to challenge himself and move to the next level. Sunida sends him to the program coordinator's office to change his class placement. During the next week, Sunida continues to observe her students' performance in class to see if any other students would benefit from moving to a different level.

3:2 Types of Assessment
3:3 Evaluation of Results
3:4 Learner Considerations

Ongoing classroom assessment: Sunida incorporates ongoing assessment tasks into her daily teaching. She gives students multiple opportunities to demonstrate their knowledge and skills through a variety of classroom assignments and formal tests. She uses information from these assessment tasks to guide her teaching.

3:2 Types of Assessment

In this class, the students are required to work on multiple drafts of three long essays. Sunida spends considerable time in class discussing with students the specific characteristics of U.S. academic rhetoric (e.g., the importance of directness and the need for supporting detail). With each essay, the students follow a well-defined writing process on topics that are closely connected to the readings and class discussions. Students do prewriting activities before writing the first draft of their essay. They bring their drafts to class and conduct peer evaluations of each other's papers. Sunida guides this peer evaluation task by giving students specific questions to consider. (Does each paragraph focus on one main idea, have a topic sentence, and provide appropriate transitions?) Sunida reads the drafts, and notes areas of improvement, focusing mainly on idea development and organization. In addition to writing comments in the students' papers, Sunida uses a scoring rubric to provide specific suggestions for revision. At this point, she schedules conferences in her office with the students who need extra help on their papers. Then, using both their peers' and Sunida's feedback, the students rewrite their essays and submit

3:1 Need for Assessment
3:2 Types of Assessment
3:4 Learner Considerations
3:5 Development and Changes

their final draft for a grade. The scoring rubric includes a section for self-assessment, so students evaluate their own work before turning in their final drafts.

Sunida also assigns short timed-writing activities for students to perform in class. These timed-writing tasks simulate the timed-writing task on the TOEFL for which students must prepare and the in-class essay exams that they will likely encounter in their college classes. Sunida coordinates the timed-writing tasks with her colleagues who teach the high-intermediate level. The instructors trade papers so they do not have to grade their own students' timed writings. The grading is done holistically, following a scale like the one used for the TOEFL.

3:1 Need for Assessment

3:2 Types of Assessment

3:4 Learner Considerations

The students in this class also engage in extensive and intensive reading activities. Sunida assigns a novel for them to read during the term. They read several chapters per week and keep a reading journal, which helps students reflect about what they are reading, practice fluency in writing, and study vocabulary systematically. Sunida asks students to divide their journals into two sections: a reading/response section and a vocabulary section. In the reading/response section, students select quotes from the week's chapters and write their opinions about the story. In the vocabulary section, the students choose 10 unknown words and write definitions and sentences. Sunida collects their journals every week and responds with short comments and questions about the content of their entries. She does not make corrections, but grades the journals (check, check-plus, check-minus) based on effort and completeness. She also creates a list of important words from the vocabulary section, which she reviews in class and uses as a test. Every week, Sunida dedicates one class session to discuss the novel and work on the vocabulary list from that week's assigned chapters.

3:2 Types of Assessment

3:5 Development and Changes

Formal tests: Instead of the typical midterm and final exams, Sunida administers four formal tests during the term. She feels that multiple tests provide information to guide her teaching and offer the students more opportunities to track their own progress. Each test includes three sections: (1) a reading passage related to the theme of the textbook chapter they are studying, with questions designed to assess the students' use of reading and writing strategies; (2) a vocabulary section that covers the vocabulary lists from the chapters of the novels and the articles they have read; and (3) a writing section that asks students to write a well-organized essay about the readings. Sunida uses information from test results to plan follow-up instruction.

At the end of the term, Sunida needs to assign a final grade to each student. Each final grade report includes extensive comments about the student's performance. Sunida reviews the formal tests and the work from all classroom assignments, including essays, timed writings, and reading journals. She also considers each student's attendance, class participation, and homework performance. She brings all this information to a faculty meeting, where the instructors discuss placement for the next term. Most students are recommended to pass to the next level, but students who are not linguistically ready to advance, because of incomplete assignments or inconsistent attendance, may be asked to repeat a level. These students are given one term of probation to work harder and make progress. In rare cases, students who have worked diligently but would benefit from another term at the same level are asked to repeat a course.

Discussion

A. Study the vignette. Make a list of the assessment tools that Sunida uses, and explain how she uses each one to plan and deliver instruction.

[Answer Key A: Answers include essays for diagnostic purposes, timed-writing tasks as preparation for the TOEFL, reading journals as reflection tools, and formal tests so students can track progress. All the assessments lead to adjustments in planning and instruction based on results. If, for example, she finds students deficient in timed writing, she prepares more TOEFL-type activities.]

B. Discuss the following:

1. The formal tests allow students to demonstrate their learning in a variety of skill areas. Discuss how the different sections of her tests are tied to the goals and content of her daily lessons.

   a. reading section

   b. vocabulary section

   c. writing section

2. Why does Sunida encourage her students to conduct peer evaluations of each other's essays? What are the benefits of this type of assessment?

C. Discuss with fellow teachers other techniques you could use to encourage peer feedback in the classroom. Then describe your ideas, comparing them to others' suggestions and explaining about how incorporating these changes could affect your instruction.

Vignette: English as a Foreign Language

Standard 3: Assessing

Background

This vignette describes the assessment practices of an instructor at North Hampshire College, a college in England that attracts adult students who come from around the globe to learn English on both short- and long-term stays. The students coming for short-term stays are referred to as "holiday students," because they typically combine 1–2 weeks of language study with tourism. The students coming for long-term stays generally spend about 3 months to prepare for the Cambridge Proficiency Examination. Although the English as a foreign language (EFL) program needs to deal differently with the assessment of these two groups of EFL students, much of the evaluation process can be similar. North Hampshire College attracts about 100 EFL students a month and provides accommodations for students to study intensively. These students are considered students of EFL because they do not intend to remain in the country and can only take advantage of the resources of the country for a short period of time.

Charles Buchanan teaches the long-term (3-month) classes. He taught for 10 years in the United States prior to teaching for 3 years in this program. He enjoys the challenge of helping students at a fast pace and seeing quick improvement. Because of the time constraints, the students are usually very motivated and work diligently. Charles likes this dynamic because he can cover a significant amount of material each day; however, he has learned that it is easy to make assumptions about student learning when moving quickly and that ongoing assessment is crucial.

Vignette

| 3:3 Evaluation of Results |

Pre-assessment surveys: Because students spend so little time at the school, the college has established a policy of identifying student needs before their arrival, with an online questionnaire that addresses goals and ambitions related to English language study, student background, and personal learning styles. With this information in hand before students arrive on campus, the instructor can make adjustments to his curriculum to ensure that the registered students will succeed.

| 3:3 Evaluation of Results |

Placement tests: Charles will probably not have more than 15 students at any given time, but the multilevel classes in this small program make it necessary to assess the language proficiency of each student in order to group them appropriately. At times he groups them by their strengths. For example, he might work on grammar with the weaker writers while the stronger writers perform a task to prepare them for the Cambridge Proficiency Examination. Charles administers a sample test that is similar to the Cambridge Proficiency Examination, and finds that in his class of 15, he would rate 10 students as low intermediate, two as high intermediate, and three as advanced in writing. He interviews each student and concludes that four students who were very strong in writing have little confidence in listening and speaking. He addresses this concern in last-minute adjustments to his lesson plans.

Ongoing classroom assessment: Most students are attending his class in order to prepare for the Cambridge Proficiency Examination, so Charles prepared his course accordingly; however, he realizes that it will be more effective to help students prepare for the test and to interact more effectively in English than merely to teach to the test. He also knows that he needs to quiz students daily on new material in order to keep them motivated. Students gain confidence when they understand expectations and are making visible progress, so Charles prepares objectives for each day of the class. He announces the objectives at the beginning of class and tests students on what they learned at the end of each session. Charles also provides a graph for students to plot their test scores to track their progress on each objective.

3:1 Need for Assessment

After a week, Charles asks students to report impressions about their progress in a class journal. This journal is a book that students can use during any class period whenever they wish, and in which Charles often writes responses to student comments. On this occasion, Charles has students write what they are not learning but feel they need to learn in the class, so he can evaluate his teaching and plan for the second week.

3:4 Learner Considerations
3:5 Development and Changes

This group needs to work on writing, so Charles provides a list of common errors that English language learners and native speakers often make, and he offers many opportunities to write essays. After returning an essay, he has students work in groups to create a peer-editing guide based on his comments so the whole class can collaborate to create a guide that they all can use in futures classes. Charles knows that assessing peers' writing will help students learn the concepts faster so they can become more critical of their own errors.

3:2 Types of Assessment
3:4 Learner Considerations

The school has also developed practice questions similar to those on the Cambridge Proficiency Examination. Charles provides the students with a practice test three times a week so students can apply new information to test-taking experiences. As a class, the instructor and students go over the test for immediate feedback. Students maintain the results of these tests, like those of the daily quizzes, on a graph that allows them to see their progress.

3:2 Types of Assessment
3:3 Evaluation of Results
3:4 Learner Considerations

Instructor/learner feedback: Charles believes that the better he knows the students, the more he can help them to learn. Every week he sets a time to interview each student and ask questions about his or her learning. He also shares observations about the student's learning styles and how he or she might best overcome challenges with English.

3:3 Evaluation of Results
3:4 Learner Considerations

Final examination: The final examination mirrors the experience students will have when they take the Cambridge Proficiency Examination. Charles discusses the results with students and makes suggestions about how they might continue to prepare on their own.

Discussion

A. The institution, the teacher, peers, or the learners themselves can do an assessment. List the different assessments that are discussed in this vignette.

Institution: _____

Teacher: _____

Peer: _____

Student (self): _____

[Answer Key A: Institution: questionnaires, practice tests; Teacher: placement test, daily quizzes, interviews; Peer: peer editing; Student: class journal, interviews with instructor]

B. Discuss the following:

1. How would these same assessments work or not work with the holiday (short-term) students?

2. Discuss other types of assessments that would be appropriate in this program.

C. If you were the instructor during the same short period, what assessments might you use? What might you do differently, and why?

Standard 4
Identity and Context

Standard 4: Identity and Context

Standard 4
Identity and Context

*Teachers understand the importance of who learners
are and how their communities, backgrounds, and
goals shape learning and expectations of learning.
Teachers recognize how context contributes to
identity formation and therefore influences learning.
Teachers use this knowledge of identity and settings
in planning, instructing, and assessing.*

Learners bring who they are—their backgrounds and experiences—to any learning situation. Adult learners in a single classroom can span many decades, bring a wide array of life experiences, and come from different sociocultural, sociopolitical, and educational backgrounds. Teachers, too, enter the classroom with a history that affects how they behave and interact, so they must consider how their own identity and background shape their understanding of their students. This reflection helps instructors to recognize the legitimacy and diversity of the identities of the adult learners with whom they are working, and to understand how these identities shape what learners do and can do in the classroom. Learners themselves may need help to make sense of their identities in a new setting, and to choose the aspects of their identities that they wish to preserve or adapt. Teachers can acknowledge students' particular needs through their actions toward and responses to learners, through the interpersonal climate of the classroom, and through the design and management of activities. The instructor must strike a delicate balance between understanding learners as people and helping them achieve their content goals in the course.

Standard 4: Identity and Context
Performance Indicators

4:1 Classroom Environment

- creates an environment conducive to adult learning

- acknowledges learners as adults

- establishes classroom routines and encourages learners' appreciation for each other

4:2 Learner Identities

- respects the legitimacy and diversity of identities and roles' impact on planning, instructing, and assessing

- uses the diversity of adult learners' identities and roles as a classroom resource

- varies instructional practices to address learner identities and roles

4:3 Instructor Interaction

- interacts equitably and responsibly with adult learners

- models respectful attitudes toward cross-cultural differences and conflicts

4:4 Learner Communities

- helps learners connect and apply their learning to home, community, and workplace

- integrates information from learners' communities in planning, instructing, and assessing

- seeks out and uses knowledge about learner communities to guide instructional practice

Vignette: Adult/Community

Standard 4: Identity and Context

Background

This vignette describes an English as a second language (ESL) adult program in northern California that takes place in a church. The community is 80% Hispanic and 10% Korean. Levels of education vary: some residents have very little formal education, a significant number have high school diplomas, and a small number hold advanced degrees. On average, seven people live in a household, and many homes house multigenerational families; 60% of the homes are apartments, and nearly all others are single-family homes.

The high-intermediate class has 25 students, 15 Hispanics and 10 Koreans. There are three students between the ages of 50 and 65, five between 40 and 50, twelve between 25 and 40, and five under 25. There are 17 married students and 8 single ones. All but five members of the class live in apartments.

Kate Jones is the instructor of this high-intermediate class. She has been teaching this particular class for 2 months and has had many successes and a few problems. Her main concern is to maintain the interest of all students during every lesson. There is no charge for this class. The students come 3 days a week in the evening, often after working a full day. She knows that if her students lose interest, they will also stop coming.

Vignette

Kate has found that giving students basic classroom responsibilities like cleaning the board, orienting new students, passing out papers, and setting up equipment helps them become more engaged and feel recognized for their efforts. She has set up a rotating schedule to encourage this type of participation. She has also learned the students' names, and makes sure she addresses each student at least once during every class. She notes publicly when students miss a class, expresses concern if they have missed several, and shows how happy she is when they return. Kate knows that it would be productive to call students who miss class and has heard of teachers having students complete postcards on the first day of class so it is easy to contact absent students. Kate has not had time for such tasks, however, so she works hard to create an inviting classroom environment, encouraging students to attend but acknowledging the many responsibilities students have outside of class and accepting when students need to miss class because of family problems or work constraints.

> 4:1 Classroom Environment
>
> 4:3 Instructor Interaction

She is required to follow the curriculum designed by the school, which includes students being able to write a complaint letter to a landlord. She is concerned about this task because five students indicated on questionnaires that they own their own home, and because she suspects that several older students are supported by their extended family. In planning the lesson about writing to a landlord, she needs to ensure that the task will be applicable for students who either do not have a landlord or do not have direct contact with one.

After wondering why this objective is so important, Kate decides that students are learning to write to a landlord, but more importantly, they are learning to identify problems in a home, to describe the problems, and to write a letter highlighting these issues. She considers ways to modify her lesson without losing the integrity of the objective. She makes a list of the following observations:

- All students live in a home with plumbing, electricity, flooring, and appliances, and all have probably experienced some kind of problem with their residences.

- Most students might have complaints related to their homes.
  — Students who rent might complain to a landlord about broken appliances or other needed repairs.

  — Students who own homes might have complaints about new appliances, or work that has been done on the home by plumbers or other contractors.

- Older and younger students who live in a home but are not responsible for its upkeep, or who do not make rent payments, may need to make requests to the person who cares and pays for the residence.

With these ideas, Kate feels more prepared to plan a lesson that is pertinent to all her students. In the presentation of the lesson, Kate tries to learn more specifics about her class and to generate interest in the task. She starts by telling a story about her home, preparing the students before she begins that she will ask them to retell the story in their own words to a partner. She recounts moving into a home with very old plumbing. When she hired a plumber to install a dishwasher, he completed the work without checking for leaks or other problems before leaving. During the night, a pipe burst and caused the kitchen and living room to flood. After the students retell the story, she asks if anyone has had a problem with plumbing. Kate has nurtured a community feeling from the beginning days of the term, and students are very comfortable discussing their problems. Three students share their experiences. She asks what other type of problems might arise in their homes, and students begin sharing their stories. During the discussion, she asks the older and younger members of the class questions to ensure their participation. Kate asks what might be done to remedy problems and makes a two-column table on the board to record ideas. The first column lists people to contact, and the students suggest landlords, the better business bureau, contractors, and family members; the second column lists possible actions, and students mention writing a letter of complaint, making phone calls, and suing.

Kate asks for help in writing a letter of complaint to the plumbing company responsible for her flood. After the letter is complete, Kate discusses the different parts of the letter. She reviews the form of a business letter and explains that the letter should include a description of the problem and a proposed solution.

Kate assumes that all her students have had housing problems and asks students to make a list of such complaints. To her surprise, three students cannot recall a single problem they have encountered. Kate thinks about asking them to list imaginary ones, but decides, instead, to have them list some of her own past problems. She offers some, of which these students can choose a few. She then asks all the students to write a personal letter of complaint to a landlord or other

4:3 Instructor Interaction

4:2 Learner Identities

4:4 Learner Communities

individual, explaining that those who do not have direct contact with landlords or contractors should write letters as if they did. The three students writing about Kate's problems will address their letters to her as if she is the landlord. Because the context was so clear, the letters turn out to be meaningful and appropriate. Kate asks the students to share their letters with a partner and imagine that the partner is the person to whom the letter was addressed. As a class, the students then share their impressions about the letters they read, commenting on their content, style, appropriateness, and clarity.

Discussion

A. Kate does several things to make students feel comfortable and to identify them as individuals. List five.

[Answer Key A: Answers include assigns classroom responsibilities, learns students' names, addresses each student every day, recognizes when students are gone, praises students, recognizes student time conflicts, adjusts activities to meets specific students' needs.]

B. Discuss the following:

1. Discuss your answers to Exercise A. How does Kate treat the students equitably? What does she do in class to help students express their individuality?

2. Kate is required to teach certain objectives. How does she make the task meaningful, even though the objectives appear not to apply to everyone in the class? How could she approach this differently?

C. Describe how you can make your classroom more inviting. What are some techniques described in the vignette that might be useful? Which of these do you consider the most important, and why?

Vignette: Workplace

Standard 4: Identity and Context

Background

This vignette describes three days of a workshop in a workplace language training program for a company of one of the largest international manufacturers of information technology. The program was designed for the internal customer service department and had a budget exceeding $100,000.

The internal customer service department works with company employees and independent contractors providing Internet connectivity and support services to small and large businesses throughout the world. Of the 120 employees in the department, 62 are native speakers of English. The remaining 58 members speak English as a second language and speak at least one additional language in addition to their native language. The internal needs analysis for the department shows that the nonnative English speakers are very knowledgeable in Internet connectivity and support services, but less than proficient with English style, word usage, and sentence structure.

The training consists of two programs. One is for the native English speakers who need business knowledge and better expertise speaking to clients from other countries, and the other is for the employees who speak English as a second language and need to develop social and speaking skills. Both programs have the specific goal of improving communication between employee and client. The instruction includes 3 hours by Internet and 3 hours in a business classroom setting. Each student works with an advisor, who assists the trainee in meeting his or her individual goals and determines the large-group seminars and small-group workshops (or lessons) that the individual needs to attend. In this way, trainees do not spend time on areas in which they have demonstrated proficiency during the pre-assessment. The trainees in the vignette that follows are being readied for a large-group seminar.

Vignette

Brad Johnson leads the introductory class for all trainees and will act as an instructor in many other workshops and certain seminars. This first meeting introduces each trainee to his or her advisor and then provides information about how to participate in the training, to access Internet seminars or workshops, to find and submit assignments, to register for live seminars or workshops, and to contact the advisor.

The live seminars and small workshops are based on subject matter identified in the needs analysis for the group, and the company has agreed to the objectives of this instruction. Brad has been given all the information gathered during the needs analysis and will use much of it as an authentic tool for creating the curriculum. Brad also works with the online developer to design online seminars and workshops, in accordance with the agreed-upon objectives. Finally, Brad also works with the advisors, who are given needs-analysis materials. These materials have a dual purpose. The overall findings help Brad design the curriculum as noted above, and they also provide information about individual trainees. The advisors act as tutors who perform specific one-on-one training, sometimes online and sometimes in person, using the individual responses of the employees to meet the exact needs of the individual trainees.

Brad conducts his first series of workshops, which are designed to support the upcoming seminars. The first seminar is entitled Productive Ways to Use the Internet in Business Settings. Because the seminars include all 120 trainees, are not geared toward the ESL students, and are broad and less interactive than the workshop lessons, Brad identifies the problem vocabulary that the trainees will encounter during the seminar and designs a lesson around the information. He finds the forms and reports that the employees may be required to use on the topic, and plans to have students use them to simulate a business model for his third, fourth, and fifth lessons. He knows the students' customer service roles in the company and divides them accordingly into groups of three to five. One student voices an objection to his grouping, stating that he would prefer to be in another group. Brad respects the student's request and allows him to change groups. Within each group, Brad encourages the members to choose roles similar to their real customer service roles in the company. Each group is charged with planning and role-playing a small business looking for ways to expand efficiently using the Internet. Brad is depending on trainees' different experiences in creating business models and expects the results of the simulation to be varied.

> 4:1 Classroom Environment
> 4:2 Learner Identities
> 4:3 Instructor Interaction
> 4:4 Learner Communities

Brad starts each class with the group as a whole. They review vocabulary and the parameters of the simulation. Next, the large group brainstorms ways the individual groups might proceed. In this discussion, Brad interweaves the vocabulary into the discussion and exhibits samples of past reports. He asks for suggestions and ideas, validating student responses by putting them all on the board. At one point, a trainee objects to another trainee's idea, claiming that the suggestion could never work and should be discounted. Brad explains that while brainstorming, all ideas are included and no idea should be judged as good or bad. He continues to list all responses on the board and then initiates a discussion on the critique.

> 4:1 Classroom Environment
> 4:2 Learner Identities
> 4:3 Instructor Interaction

The needs analysis suggests that trainees have problems using the conditional in writing and speaking tasks, so Brad teaches students how to use it appropriately and follows the presentation with exercises in the context of the simulation. He demonstrates how the conditional will be used when brainstorming and discussing as a group. As students produce ideas, they naturally will use this structure, and Brad encourages the trainees to be mindful of it as they work in their groups.

In the first of the three classes, Brad gives the students a step-by-step process paper that explains the steps of the simulation:

1. Identify your company name, what you produce, your target customers, the size of your company (number of employees, etc.), and your annual gross sales projections. Write a report including this information.

2. Identify the specific Internet resources you choose to use for your company and what new employees you may need to hire.

3. Identify the cost of such a venture and the risk in pursuing the approach.

4. Identify obstacles and challenges. What resources from our company can be used to help this business be successful?

5. Using the forms provided, develop a cost/benefit analysis of expanding the business using the Internet resources that you have identified.

6. Write a report and prepare an oral presentation for the group about your conclusions.

The instructor is available to help a particular group or to redirect the whole class while the groups are researching and writing their reports (Step 1). During the 3-day workshop, the students have used authentic forms, reinforced their knowledge of company procedures, worked with relevant vocabulary and subject matter, and analyzed existing reports in order to develop English proficiency in the context of their work. Brad has prepared them for the next step—the seminar.

Discussion

A. Study the vignette. List evidence of Brad's efforts to create an environment conducive to adult learning and to acknowledge his learners as adults.

[Answer Key A: Answers include the needs analyses helps Brad recognize and develop plans based on employee needs; students' objections are taken seriously, and adjustments are made; and Brad depends on employees' experience in the field for many activities.]

B. Discuss the following:

1. Do you think this model of developing a project by which students learn specific roles and responsibilities would be effective? These types of activities are sometimes referred to as team projects. Can you imagine this team project approach in other situations? Brainstorm ideas of other team projects that might be effective.

2. Discuss how this lesson will allow learners to connect and apply their learning to the workplace. The learners are not business owners but employees in customer service. What benefit, if any, is there to having them do a cost/benefit analysis or participate in such an activity?

C. In an adult classroom, a student may occasionally make requests or demands that are inappropriate or unusual. Think of a few examples of possible disruptions of this sort. How would you deal with these problems?

Vignette: College/University

Standard 4: Identity and Context

Background

This vignette takes place at a large urban community college in Florida. The college has eight campuses and a variety of ESL programs to meet the needs of community education (vocational and recreational ESL) and English for academic purposes (EAP) students. The EAP programs serve close to 9,000 students and constitute more than 17% of the total credit enrollment at the college. The majority of the students enrolled in EAP classes intend to earn a 2-year associate's degree. At a minimum, EAP students need to have a high school diploma, and many have some education beyond high school, albeit often interrupted. About 5% of the students are considered Generation 1.5; that is, they spent some time in the U.S. school system and completed high school in the United States rather than in their native countries. This minority evidences skills as "ear learners," because they have strong oral and social skills but also have gaps in their academic preparation that affect reading, writing, and critical expression. Nonetheless, the majority of the EAP students have relatively strong academic backgrounds from their native countries, but their English limitations put them at a disadvantage in U.S. higher education. They are immigrant residents who intend to remain in the United States and contribute to the social fabric of this country.

The advanced class described below meets at a campus located in a neighborhood known as Little Havana. All of the students speak Spanish as a first language, and most are from Cuba. Other countries represented are Nicaragua, Colombia, Venezuela, and Argentina. There are 28 students, 18 female and 10 male. Most are in their twenties, study full time, have jobs, and live with extended family members in modest, often crowded settings.

Mariah Miner is the instructor for this advanced reading class and has taught the class many times. Her goals are to prepare the students for an exam on general reading comprehension that they must take prior to registering for freshman-level college courses and to help them become effective readers of freshman-level college material.

Vignette

Close to the end of a 16-week term, the students are studying the last chapter of an ESL textbook that presents academic reading selections from popular freshman-level courses. The discipline area for this chapter is education, and the readings are about the world roots of U.S. education. Students explore identity, personal beliefs, values, and educational theories in a guided manner as they work with the chapter.

Mariah begins with a warm-up discussion and journal assignment. She asks the students questions such as "Have you ever thought about becoming a teacher?" and "Would you prefer teaching children or adults?" Then she introduces the idea that we are all teachers at times, because teaching occurs not only at school, but also at home and in workplaces. Then the students freewrite for 10 minutes about their thoughts on teaching and education.

4:1 Classroom Environment

4:2 Learner Identities

| 4:1 Classroom Environment |

Mariah structures her students' learning experiences during this chapter to include a field study, reading and analysis, multiple-choice practice tests, reading application exercises, and reading for cultural consciousness. Throughout the work with this chapter, she offers students many choices leading to personally relevant learning experiences.

| 4:1 Classroom Environment |

Field study: In order to arrange for a class observation opportunity for her students, Mariah investigates which general education courses are being offered at the same time as her class. For this term, they include Biology, Critical Thinking/Ethics, Introduction to Education, Introduction to Computers, and Introduction to Sociology. She arranges with the professors of these classes to have students observe, so her students can choose a course based on their interests and course requirements for an associate's degree. Each student receives a copy of the syllabus and a link to a Web-based reading assignment for the course he or she will observe. Her ESL students are excited to be able to experience a "regular" college class. Prior to the visits, they wonder about presentation style and the behavior of the other students. Will they be able to understand the professor? Will the students participate? Will some of them have accents? Will they take notes?

| 4:2 Learner Identities |
| 4:3 Instructor Interaction |

During the first EAP class meeting after the observation, Mariah plans a debriefing with all students. Students share positive commentary about their visits and compare their experiences in a U.S. college class to classes they have taken in their native countries and to ESL classes. They generally feel excitement about the instructional content and dynamics that they witnessed, and several students find that the experience of sitting in an academic college class helps them imagine taking such a class in the near future.

| 4:3 Instructor Interaction |

Reading and analysis: The next assignment involves reading a selection about education in preliterate societies and in ancient China. Students are reminded to apply a strategy they have learned for reading academic textbook passages called muscle reading. It includes three phases: (1) preview, outline, and question; (2) read, underline, and answer; and (3) recite, review, and review again. The reading selection teaches students about educational practices from ancient times that still influence practices in the 21st century. For example, in preliterate times, storytelling and learning through song were common, especially among young children. The practice of administering national exams, which is still valued in many world societies, developed in ancient China. Students discuss the benefits and drawbacks of such exams and share experiences from other countries.

| 4:3 Instructor Interaction |

Practice multiple-choice tests: Mariah segues from this discussion into practice exercises for standardized multiple-choice reading comprehension exams, first with questions about the education passage the students have just read, and then with a variety of shorter passages with questions that are more like the reading comprehension exam the students will soon take. She provides handouts with practice exams, information about tutoring support on campus, and many additional links to practice tests and testing advice that she has found online.

| 4:4 Learner Communities |

Reading application exercises: The next reading assignment is an in-depth chart that provides an historical overview of 10 influential periods in education. The students learn about chart-reading strategies, and then work with the information in the chart. First, as a class, they create a timeline on the board to show the chronological space covered by the 10 periods. Then, they work in nine small groups to prepare oral summaries about each period. For each historical period, one group needs to explain who the students were, who their teachers were, the subjects they studied, how they learned, and any practices from those times that continue to influence educational practices today. Within the small groups, the students agree on individual roles, such as recorder, reporter, information seekers, and English monitor. They prepare an index card for the reporter with notes for the oral summary, and then someone from each of the nine groups presents the group's findings to the whole class.

The final reading selection is about education in India and ancient Egypt. Near the end, the text proposes a controversial theory about the possible strong tie between Egypt and ancient Greece. A historical researcher cited in the selection claims that Western culture associated with Greece is actually rooted in North Africa. This provides an effective opportunity for a class discussion on theories of inclusion in education, and how across time, the U.S. system has moved toward a goal of inclusion because diversity and pluralism are valued. A consciousness-raising look around the classroom, and a further look around the college campus and immediate neighborhood, all serve to illustrate the reality of diversity being an integral part of the community.

4:2 Learner Identities

4:4 Learner Communities

Discussion

A. Study the vignette. Number the following activities from 1 to 5 and think about how the sequence illustrates a progression of understanding and facilitates critical thinking.

____ multiple-choice practice tests

____ reading and analysis

____ reading application exercises

____ reading for cultural consciousness

____ field study

[Answer Key A: 3-2-4-5-1]

B. Discuss the following:

1. Identify Mariah's student population and discuss three ways her lessons evidence attention to identity and context.

2. How does the instructor help students apply what they have learned to the real world? Discuss more ways she could have done this.

C. Select one of the activities incorporated by the instructor. Explain how you could try something similar in your own class setting. How would you structure the activity? How would you address elements of identity and context?

Vignette: Intensive English

Standard 4: Identity and Context

Background

This vignette describes University Preparation, a course offered in an intensive English program (IEP) at a large public university in Arizona. The course is an elective offering for low-advanced students who intend to pursue a college degree in the United States. The students spend 3 hours per week in the ESL class and an additional 3 hours observing a university course of their choice. Under the guidance of the ESL instructor, the students choose a class that is related to their future academic major and then obtain the professor's permission to observe it. As unregistered students, they attend lectures and take notes but do not complete assignments or take tests for the university course. The parallel ESL class covers topics such as orientation to university procedures, development of cross-cultural awareness, academic adjustment, and improvement of language skills such as listening and note-taking. Because this is an elective class, students receive a pass/fail grade based on participation and completion of assignments in the ESL class, and attendance and note-taking in the university course.

David Correa is the instructor of this class, which has 23 students, 13 female and 10 male. They come from nine different countries: South Korea (eight students), Japan (four students), Taiwan (four students), Thailand (two students), France (one student), Indonesia (one student), Mexico (one student), Saudi Arabia (one student), and the United Arab Emirates (one student). There are 13 undergraduates and 10 graduate students, and they are majoring in such academic disciplines as soil science, international business, and chemical engineering.

Vignette

4:1 Classroom Environment

David organizes a variety of activities for the class. Many of the activities surround the college classes that the students are observing. The students work on study skills such as techniques for note-taking, listening to lectures to remember information, and reading textbooks. David also invites as guest speakers both an international student advisor, who gives a presentation on academic adjustment problems, and an expert in international admissions, who discusses application procedures and regulations. In addition, David invites four of his former students who are now enrolled in the university to answer questions about their experiences transitioning from the intensive English program to the university. They discuss topics such as course workload, grading procedures, and relationships with professors. David establishes a routine in the class, so most students know what to expect and come to class eager to learn. The students who are chronically late need to discipline themselves so they can be successful in a university setting; David advises and encourages them to come on time, and they eventually recognize that they are missing important concepts by arriving late and that they are also disrupting the rest of the class.

4:1 Classroom Environment

4:2 Learner Identities

In addition to organizing activities of general interest, David individualizes instruction. On the first day of class, after personal introductions, David gives the students a questionnaire about their educational backgrounds and future academic goals. The information obtained from the questionnaire gives David a concrete idea of the diverse needs of his students. A few of the graduate students have already achieved a high Test of English as a Foreign Language (TOEFL) score and have definite ideas about the universities where they would like to study; some have even contacted prospective professors and discussed their academic plans. Most of the students, however, have not yet attained their desired TOEFL score and are unsure of how to approach the university application process. Two students have very low high school grade point averages from their home countries, which indicates that they might benefit from studying at a community college for 1 or 2 years before transferring to a 4-year institution.

David knows that this is a time of transition and uncertainty for his students. Many of them are feeling pressure from their families or from sponsoring agencies to pass the TOEFL and to be accepted into a college. One of David's objectives in this class is to ease this pressure by guiding students through an examination of their own academic credentials, an evaluation of their future goals, and an investigation of institutions that match their qualifications and interests. David starts this process by leading students to clarify their values through an exercise that helps them identify aspects of a college that are important to them (location, size, quality of academic programs, cost, climate, etc.). Through this activity he learns, for example, that one student feels strongly about studying at a Christian institution, and that another student is considering only one college because his father studied there. Cost is a deciding factor for some of the students, but climate is more important for others. After the students have identified their own priorities, David spends several sessions with the class in the computer lab and guides them through Internet searches of institutions that match their qualifications and preferences. By the end of the course, each student has found at least two institutions of interest and has researched thoroughly the admission requirements of those schools.

> 4:2 Learner Identities
>
> 4:3 Instructor Interaction

In addition to helping students solidify their academic goals, David addresses cultural issues related to college life. Throughout the course, the students participate in an online discussion about the university class they are attending. Weekly discussions include topics such as observations about interactions between students and the professor in class, comparisons between classroom behavior in the United States and in the home country, and personal experiences and feelings about communicating with U.S. classmates. After students respond to David's initial questions, they engage in dialogue by responding to each other's comments. David also provides feedback on the students' remarks and poses questions for further reflection. This online discussion gives students prolonged opportunities for reflection on their observation experience and their academic futures. The Web format also makes class participation more balanced because it allows students who feel somewhat uncomfortable expressing their opinions in a face-to-face format to participate equally with their more outspoken classmates.

> 4:4 Learner Communities

When David moves the lessons beyond the academic goals to a discussion of what the students will do once they have obtained their degrees, he is amazed to learn that many learners have few ideas. David realizes that the students will better apply their learning, and that their academic goals will be more meaningful, if they have a career in mind as they work toward their degrees. He modifies instruction somewhat to include a conversation about possible careers. The discussions about careers become an ongoing part of the course.

> 4:2 Learner Identities

Discussion

A. Read the vignette. One of David's goals for this course is to ease the pressure his students feel during their transition between the intensive English program and future degree programs. List five ways he accomplished this goal.

[Answer Key A: Answers include uses guest speakers to prepare students, invites past students to describe their experiences, helps students clarify their goals, guides students through Internet searches, initiates discussions about cultural issues that students might encounter.]

B. Discuss the following:

1. David uses the diversity of his students' identities as a classroom resource. Describe at least two ways he does this.

2. David encourages his students to engage in self-reflection and collaborative reflection about their own educational experiences, feelings about further study, and expectations about their academic futures. Do you agree that this type of reflection is beneficial to students? Why or why not?

C. Discuss how you can create an environment conducive to adult learning in your own classroom. How would you find out more about your students? How might this information about the individual needs of your students change the way you teach?

Vignette: English as a Foreign Language

Standard 4: Identity and Context

Background

This vignette describes an English as a foreign language (EFL) college in Australia that accepts young adults from all over the world. The students described in this vignette are from China, Japan, Korea, the Philippines, Scandinavia, South America, Switzerland, and Thailand. Typically, students come for a 4-week program and then travel and sightsee in Australia. They are all at an intermediate level and have been prescreened by a basic assessment tool that identifies language levels for placement purposes but does not differentiate between learning styles, educational experience, or any other factors.

Ann Brighton teaches the intermediate class. The main objective of the class is to help students develop speaking skills. Most of the students Ann teaches are particularly interested in speaking well enough to communicate with Australians while visiting the country. The program is organized by theme, and the vignette below recounts part of the unit on friends and relationships. This vignette is about two different sections of the same class. Both classes are based on an article in the textbook about dating, sex before marriage, and homosexuality. Ann recognizes the importance of treating these sensitive subjects differently depending on her audience.

Vignette

Class 1: Ann Brighton has 17 students for whom she establishes a general routine, which includes journal writing as a warm-up to allow students to establish goals and generate ideas for later discussions, class discussion to introduce a role-play, and finally, group discussion. Ann knows that students learn much more quickly if she presents information that interests them, so she asks for continuous feedback on how the class should proceed. She asks different students to lead class discussions each day, and she respects all ideas by placing them on the board even when she disagrees with them. For the most part, Ann stays neutral during discussions and intervenes only to advance the conversations or to help students express themselves.

> 4:1 Classroom Environment

All the students in the class know one another. They have been in the program before and feel comfortable speaking about their beliefs. They are not intimidated by one another, but some members of the group can become emotional about their differing points of view. The group is studying the textbook unit entitled Friends and Relationships. The textbook provides a reading that allows students to weigh pros and cons. During the class about sex before marriage, two members of the group in particular have very strong opinions, and a somewhat heated discussion ensues. Ann also has strong feelings about these issues, but tries to allow students to voice their opinions without intimidating or influencing them. Ultimately, Ann needs to step in and bring the discussion back to the reading. She decides that this would be a good topic to debate at the following class meeting, and she adjusts her lesson plan to provide time for such an event. Ann decides that, to help students see other students' perspectives, she will ask a few to present the point of view that they do not hold. Four students agree to do this, and the entire class participates at the next class in a debate that is moderated by the instructor. The debate allows a

> 4:1 Classroom Environment
>
> 4:2 Learner Identities
>
> 4:4 Learner Communities

much more controlled environment, and students are able to focus on facts and ideas with less emotion than in the previous discussion. After the debate, the class debriefs and moves on to the next topic.

4:1 Classroom Environment

4:2 Learner Identities

4:4 Learner Communities

Class 2: This class of 24 is an interesting mix of students. Each class is different, and Ann knows that she must identify student needs in order to teach effectively. The women appear much less willing to speak than their male counterparts, so Ann realizes that she must approach the unit on relationships differently than she did in the previous class. The students are all single and in their twenties, so Ann plans to facilitate a 15-minute discussion in small groups on the characteristics of a perfect relationship as a prereading activity to prepare students for the article on sex before marriage in the textbook. She understands that the Asian women may feel embarrassed by discussing relationships in front of the men, so she assigns the women and men to separate groups, three small groups of women and three of men. She attempts to make each group as diverse as possible, with as many countries as possible represented in each group. She asks each group to appoint a leader to keep the members on task and encourage participation from each member. Each group will also have a timer, a reporter (to report the characteristics listed in each group), and a secretary.

4:2 Learner Identities

4:4 Learner Communities

After the secretaries have written all the characteristics on paper and the reporter shares the information with the class, the groups then reconvene and rank the characteristics they listed in order of importance. The teacher emphasizes at the beginning of this exercise that there is no right answer and that each person should defend his or her point of view, but that each group should attempt to agree on one specific ranking. Groups are given an additional 15 minutes to do this. The teacher then randomly asks each group to provide information about some of the arguments and how they ranked the characteristics. The final part of the lesson includes language feedback identifying students' common and individual errors.

On the second day, Ann reviews the discussion from the previous day and asks students to write their impressions in their journals. Then she asks them to read the article on sex before marriage in the textbook. Ann again divides the class into six, but this time she assigns mixed-sex groups. This particular reading is not personal to the students, so Ann believes they will be more comfortable discussing the issues.

Discussion

A. Study the vignette. List the significant differences in the way Ann approached the two classes. Why did Ann treat the two classes differently?

[Answer Key A: She was more careful with Class 2 because of the dynamics with the sex and nationality of the students, whereas she could be more flexible with Class 1 because they all knew one another. She felt it necessary to prepare Class 2 more for the reading because of the class dynamics.]

B. Discuss the following:

1. What strategies might EFL teachers use to overcome the sensitivities of students due to such factors as sex and nationality?

2. Do you think EFL students should be encouraged to use English in situations that may cause them discomfort? Why or why not?

C. Ann treated the two classes in different ways. Her desire to meet student needs made it necessary for her to plan two sets of lessons instead of just one. Explain how you might make the task of creating two lesson plans for one topic more manageable.

Standard 5 Language Proficiency

Standard 5: Language Proficiency

Standard 5
Language Proficiency

Teachers demonstrate proficiency in social, business/ workplace, and academic English. Proficiency in speaking, listening, reading, and writing means that a teacher is functionally equivalent to a native speaker with some higher education.

It is important for teachers to be good language models for their students. Teachers must be able to

- speak English with sufficient accuracy and fluency to participate effectively in formal and informal communication on a variety of topics (e.g., practical, social, professional)
- handle complicated social tasks such as elaborating, complaining, and apologizing
- narrate, describe, and link sentences together smoothly
- support their opinions, explain content in detail, and hypothesize on topics with which they are familiar

Teachers of adult language learners should also be able to

- demonstrate language strategies for effective interaction with others, such as encouraging others to participate and resolving conflicts
- show an awareness of discourse strategies, such as distinguishing main ideas from supporting detail, paraphrasing, and circumlocuting
- demonstrate control of suprasegmental features of English (i.e., pitch, stress, intonation)
- communicate orally and in writing with a variety of stakeholders using the appropriate registers. Such stakeholders may include government agencies, colleagues, nonteaching staff, and other stakeholders.
- read a variety of genres, including government communications, institutional memos, Web pages, fiction and nonfiction books, and periodicals
- model effective reading strategies for their learners
- advocate on behalf of nonnative-English-speaking teachers (either themselves or colleagues) and address any student concerns regarding an issue
- model cultural aspects of English (e.g., personal space, gestures, body language) appropriate to various environments

Standard 5: Language Proficiency Performance Indicators

5:1 General Proficiency

- demonstrates proficiency in oral, written, and professional English
- demonstrates proficiency in social, academic, and professional English

5:2 Other Contexts

- demonstrates familiarity with more than one variety of English
- varies register according to context

5:3 Classroom Performance

- serves as an English language model for learners

5:4 Nonnative Advocate

- explains and advocates for NNES teachers

Vignette: Adult/Community

Standard 5: Language Proficiency

Background

This vignette is about the experiences of an instructor from Brazil who teaches at a large adult school in Florida. The school has an extensive English as a second language (ESL) program whose primary goal is to encourage students to develop skills that will help them be successful in college programs. The school maintains high standards for the students and rigid language proficiency requirements for their teachers. Isabel Andrade was hired three years ago. She speaks English quite well and her education is adequate for the position, but she had concerns during her interview because she speaks with an accent and had heard of applicants who did not qualify because their English could not be understood or they were considered poor models of English. Every teacher at her school is observed and evaluated once a year, so she knows she has been performing well. Moreover, the school administrator has been giving her additional responsibilities, so Isabel is becoming increasingly confident that her language skills are more than adequate for this position.

Vignette

Isabel's first assignment at the school is to teach the lowest level students in the program. She worries that the administration may have doubts about her abilities, so she makes efforts to prove to the administration, to her students, and to herself that she is a good teacher. She realizes that low-level students in particular need a good model, because many are nervous about venturing beyond their local family and the community where their native language is regularly spoken. The administration begins to see that Isabel has much to offer because she is so aware of her English. She teaches students pronunciation by modeling and occasionally by instruction, and she works especially with intonation and rhythm. She is able to relate to her students' difficulties, because she once experienced similar issues learning English, even though no student in her class is from Brazil or speaks Portuguese as a first language.

> 5:1 General Proficiency
> 5:3 Classroom Performance

After two semesters, the administration has given Isabel a new teaching assignment, the advanced workplace/business ESL class, because she has business experience in Brazil. She will be teaching students correct formal language for interviews and business letters. Her experience and education pay off, and she is recognized as a good teacher; however, she finds the assignment quite challenging. She learns that certain aspects of rhetoric are different in the United States than in Brazil and has to study on her own to prepare for the class. She also discovers that, although she speaks English quite well and understands English grammar better than many nonnative speakers because she had to learn it as an adult, she has allowed certain idioms and forms of informal speech to creep into her language. She needs to make a distinction for herself between formal and informal speech so she does not unintentionally teach language that would be inappropriate for a workplace/business course.

> 5:1 General Proficiency
> 5:2 Other Contexts
> 5:3 Classroom Performance

Isabel becomes actively involved in the ESL curriculum-writing process at her school. Because of her particular experience and background, she has many ideas to contribute, the teachers learn to appreciate her opinions, and she becomes a trusted instructor and member of the ESL department.

5:4 Nonnative Advocate

The school does not change its rigid proficiency requirements for teachers; in fact, Isabel is the first nonnative speaker they have hired. Isabel's success as a teacher demonstrates that there are many benefits to hiring some nonnative speakers with proficiency in English. Isabel worries that certain good nonnative English speakers have been overlooked in the interviewing process for new teachers. She begins to attend the department meetings and regularly suggests that the administration establish a list of criteria in order to make more objective decisions about applicants' English proficiency.

Discussion

A. Study the vignette. ESL instructors whose first language is not English have challenges that native English speakers do not have. Make a list of the challenges that Isabel faced in this vignette and describe how she overcame them.

[Answer Key A: Answers may include: She believed the administration had doubts about her; she makes extra effort to meet student needs; she recognizes a difference between U.S. and Brazilian rhetoric; she studies to learn more about it; she tends to use informal English that is not appropriate for business and has to monitor her English more.]

B. Discuss the following:

1. According to Standard 5, language proficiency is important in overall teacher performance. What can a nonnative speaker do to improve his or her chances of getting a teaching position?

2. How did Isabel demonstrate her value to the school administrators and the department? What particular experience did Isabel have that served to enrich the program?

C. The issue of being a good model for language learning is complex. What makes a good model? Study the narrative and performance indicators for Standard 5. Discuss what being a good model means to you and others at your institution.

Vignette: Workplace

Standard 5: Language Proficiency

Background

This vignette describes a program for new law school graduates who are nonnative English speakers and have all just started work in a large multinational legal firm with headquarters in the United States. Although the passive language level of these trainees is extremely high, they have not developed a competent style of writing for the professional law workplace. This legal firm requires its employees to write well in order to preserve the image of the organization.

Before the firm instituted the workplace program, clients had complained about the writing mistakes they had discovered in the firm's letters. Some of these clients even questioned the legal competence of the lawyers because of their inability to write correct informational letters. The firm took these concerns seriously and decided to develop and implement intensive writing workshops for all newly hired lawyers within the organization. The instructor is Anita Mendez. She is a skilled professional from Bolivia and has prepared extensively to qualify for such an assignment.

Vignette

Anita Mendez, the instructor of this program and a lawyer herself, is confident in her understanding of the form and content of legal information letters. She has a sample letter from each of the students and notices that most of them muddy their writing with difficult words and unnecessarily complicated grammar. She selects a range of legal information letters to share with the trainees as models, and starts class by asking the trainees to identify the generic structure of one such letter, and then to examine particular linguistic features. She explains to the students that the writing is very formal, but that the letter should include neither lofty language nor jargon.

| 5:1 General Proficiency |
| 5:3 Classroom Performance |

Anita then has the trainees revise their own letters with the express purpose of clarifying and simplifying where necessary. She also introduces to the class the basic principles of a writing technique called Plain English. Using this technique, the writer considers the readers' needs and avoids unnecessary jargon that can detract from the message. Anita follows the lecture with a discussion about how important this is in legal writing. The students trust Anita's linguistic expertise, her knowledge of the law, and her understanding of effective letter writing.

| 5:3 Classroom Performance |

After class, Anita finds time in the lunchroom to discuss her approach with the office managers and the chief executive officer (CEO). They have hired Anita but are not confident that she can help their employees. They do not question Anita's accent because they know that she has a substantial amount of expertise in the law and they understand her without effort. Anita has a certificate in teaching English to speakers of others languages (TESOL) in addition to a law degree, and she understands the benefits as well as the challenges to being a nonnative-English-speaking teacher. She has decided that she enjoys teaching more than law, but in this environment she can do both.

| 5:2 Other Contexts |

5:2 Other
Contexts

The CEO asks her questions about the class. Although she has had several formal meetings with him in the past in his office, he is friendlier at lunch. They converse about her plans for the class, and he seems satisfied but asks her to document her progress in weekly reports.

The next day, Anita introduces a more complex letter to the class and asks the students to work in pairs to analyze it. She then gives them a similarly complex task to write collaboratively as a team. During this time, Anita walks around the classroom, making corrections and providing extra input where necessary. After the employees complete the task, she reviews the letters. At the next class meeting, Anita helps the class correct the letters by projecting examples of what the teams have written on a screen.

5:3 Classroom
Performance

As requested by the CEO, Anita writes a report upon completing the first week. She views this task as essential for the continuation, and therefore the success, of the course. She is a competent writer, reviews her work scrupulously, and submits a formal and well-crafted report to the CEO. Anita also writes a quick thank-you note to the CEO for entrusting her with the work she is doing for his company and to express that she feels confident in her ability to show marked improvement in just a few weeks.

5:2 Other
Contexts

After several weeks, Anita shows students an example of a letter they might receive from a client. She asks them to apply both their knowledge of the subject matter and their new writing skills to respond to the letter. When she compares their new work to the sample letters they wrote before the course began, she notices marked improvement. She is encouraged that, even before she has addressed the concept of circular rhetoric, the students' efforts to simplify their writing also led them to write more directly.

5:2 Other
Contexts

Discussion

A. Study the vignette. List the different ways Anita demonstrated her ability to speak and write in a variety of contexts and to change register.

[Answer Key A: Answers may include classroom instruction, weekly reports, and thank-you notes.]

B. Discuss the following:

1. What evidence can you cite that Anita has sufficient proficiency to conduct this course? Are areas other than language proficiency important in this course?

2. How does a person assess how formally to speak to a boss or supervisor? Who makes that decision in discourse?

C. What is more important in your present teaching position, appropriate and clear speaking skills or appropriate writing skills? If most of your instruction involved speaking and listening, why would appropriate writing skills still be essential?

Vignette: College/University

Standard 5: Language Proficiency

Background

This vignette takes place at a medium-sized urban community college in Georgia (United States). The college has three campuses with ESL programs designed for students who intend to pursue associate's degrees upon completing a three-level series of ESL coursework. The programs serve more than 1,500 ESL students. Many of the students arrived in the United States before completing secondary (and sometimes elementary) education in their home countries, so their levels of academic preparation and exposure to academic materials in English vary.

The ESL department at the main college campus has seven full-time faculty members, including one who is originally from Odessa, Ukraine. Among the seven faculty members, Elena is the only nonnative speaker of English, and she is the newest addition to the faculty. Some of the other faculty members come from minority backgrounds, including one African American and one Hispanic American, but both of these individuals were born in the United States. Unlike those instructors, Elena faced challenges in learning English. After studying English as a foreign language (EFL) in Ukraine, she still needed to study ESL and then English in the United States in order to prepare herself for teaching. She worked her way through a community college and then a university, eventually earning a master's degree in TESOL. Elena had many experiences in her first teaching positions that prepared her for her full-time position. These experiences also served as encouragement for her to return to school to earn a master's degree. The vignette briefly describes her efforts and then discusses her full-time position.

Now that she has been hired to teach at a community college, Elena will need to demonstrate exemplary instructional performance as well as professional contributions such as presentations and publications in her tenure portfolio. For professional development, she will need to take a required course with the other new faculty hired in all disciplines during the same year. She feels confident and challenged, has high expectations for herself, and wants to be an effective model for her students as well as a respected colleague among her faculty peers.

Vignette

Elena's first teaching job in the United States was at a Montessori school, and after earning her bachelor's degree, she taught full time for 1 year at a high school. While teaching at the high school, she also taught ESL evening and summer courses to adults at the community college. At the community college she quickly felt at ease as an instructor, and appreciated by her students. They expressed great enthusiasm about her classes, and she knew she was making a difference. Any doubts she may have had about her English were assuaged.

It was at the community college that she learned the value of being more than prepared for her classes and would sometimes presketch her blackboard plan on a note card. When teaching grammar, for example, she would study the material in the textbook carefully before class to plan her explanations and anticipate student questions. She would think deeply about grammar

5:1 General Proficiency
5:3 Classroom Performance

points that had been challenging for her as a second language learner. She remembered being unable to detect the difference between the present perfect and the simple past when learning ESL. As a teacher, she tried to explain this distinction clearly, share many examples, and provide numerous opportunities for practice, including many interactive activities. She also researched grammar games in language magazines and teacher reference books to bring the topic to life.

5:1 General Proficiency

5:2 Other Contexts

Although Elena loved her work at the community college, a year after she was hired part time the institution began to require a master's degree in TESOL. She was not happy about being unable to continue as an adjunct, but this policy change was an impetus for her to pursue graduate-level studies at the university. Returning to the university as a graduate student increased her confidence in her English and allowed her to focus on classes that were meaningful to her ESL teaching career. Her graduate school experience was unlike her undergraduate education, during which she had taken required general courses, such as oceanography, that she found difficult because she lacked the language skills to understand the reading and lectures. As a TESOL master's student, she felt more comfortable; she contributed experiences, observations, and reflections to class discussions; and she wrote successful research papers. In certain ways, English was becoming more dominant than her native Russian. For instance, Elena sensed that she could now read English more quickly than Russian.

5:2 Other Contexts

5:3 Classroom Performance

After earning her master's degree, Elena again taught some part-time classes for the community college. Soon thereafter, she was interviewed and offered a full-time position. After nearly a year on the faculty there, she continues to prepare thoroughly for her classes, and views this as a priority. She is also an active member of her department, serving on three committees and accepting the role of cochair for a special committee that will organize a daylong event celebrating all the countries represented by students at the college and the United Nations. Last semester, she gave a public presentation in English for the first time, participating in two panels during the college's professional development conference. She felt nervous before speaking but wanted to share what she had learned because public speaking brings recognition and pride. In addition, Elena wrote an online article about teaching reading for her department's electronic newsletter, and she contributed to developing grammar materials that will be part of a grant-funded writing lab. She is also excited to have learned how to develop online course materials for her classes.

5:4 Nonnative Advocate

At this point, Elena feels quite satisfied with her position, and she is optimistic about her opportunities. She also recognizes her distinctive contributions as a nonnative-English-speaking (NNES) teacher and has become actively involved in promoting understanding about the topic to her colleagues. Teaching English, Elena's own second language, has enriched both her life and the lives of her students and colleagues.

Discussion

A. Elena's self-assessment portfolio will serve her as a vehicle for reflection and demonstrate to her department her value as a faculty member. Select three aspects of Elena's vignette that you think would be most important for her to include in her self-assessment and explain why.

[Answer Key A: Answers will vary.]

B. Discuss the following:

1. Discuss how Elena's English proficiency has continued to evolve. What language aspects do you think would be most challenging for her? What steps has she actively taken to continue to improve her command of English?

2. How do you think being active in the department helped Elena? Discuss other such opportunities that instructors might find.

C. Have you taken a course in any subject with an instructor who is not a native speaker of the language of instruction? Discuss your experiences. How does language proficiency affect instruction?

Vignette: Intensive English

Standard 5: Language Proficiency

Background

This vignette describes an intensive English program (IEP) in the United States. The students come from all over the world, including Colombia, Japan, Korea, mainland China, Mexico, Taiwan, and Venezuela. The IEP is connected to a private university in a medium-sized town on the west coast of the United States. Many of the students are in the United States to pursue either a bachelor's or a master's degree. As is true in many intensive programs, the students have high expectations and are usually prepared to work hard. There are four levels in the program, ranging from beginning to advanced-intermediate, and the levels are generally well coordinated. There are usually two projects during each session that integrate reading, writing, and oral communication with appropriate grammatical structures. Sandy Chang is a new teacher in the program and has been asked to teach the intermediate oral communication skills class. This class meets for 50 minutes, five times a week. Sandy is from Taiwan and teaches at the English Language Center (ELC). She has just received her master's in TESOL and is eager to use her professional work visa to spend the next 6 months teaching in this quality program before returning home.

Vignette

The ELC has only recently offered paid teaching positions to the NNES teachers in the program. So far, there have been mixed reactions. Some of the NNES teachers have been successful with the students, but others have had their pronunciation, vocabulary, and grammar knowledge challenged. Sandy is concerned about being a nonnative speaker but welcomes the challenge. She has 5 years of teaching experience in Taiwan and believes that it is essential to radiate confidence.

All of the courses in this program are integrated, so Sandy knows she will be teaching reading, writing, and grammar. Each level involves a major learning project. Currently, she is working on a biography project that involves all of the teachers in various capacities. As the listening and speaking teacher, Sandy sets up interviews with various members in the community, including some people at the university. Sandy is responsible for making the first connection with the community members. After seeking advice from some of the seasoned teachers, she makes initial inquiries to identify people who might be willing to be interviewed about their lives by ESL students. She has success until one potential interviewee politely suggests that the questions are far too personal and that Sandy may not understand "U.S. ways." Sandy finds this accusation odd, because she finds U.S. residents far too personal. She explains that this is an opportunity for growth and mutual understanding among the ELC students and the community alike. Ultimately, the woman agrees to participate.

Sandy takes another perplexing phone call the following day from a professor she studied with and admired while at the university as an undergraduate. The faculty member wonders if this assignment will help students with their language proficiency. If ESL students are preparing for academic work, he feels that they should spend much more time reading and writing. Having endured an English program in her own country that consisted mostly of translating English texts, she asserts confidently that enjoyment and motivation augment students' language proficiency, and that this activity is closely linked to reading and writing because the students will read and write biographies as a final outcome of the project. She explains that students are preparing for college and need an orientation to the campus and culture. He is swayed by her argument and becomes eager to help.

5:1 General Proficiency

Next, Sandy prepares a detailed handout outlining the project so that students can begin working. She thinks it through carefully, anticipating the problems students may confront. Most of them have never interviewed someone, so they need to have their questions prepared in advance. They also need to learn to ask openers, follow-up questions, and closers. Having completed this project herself as an ESL student, Sandy understands the problems that students may encounter and the skills needed for interviewing. She also realizes that students will need a model, and she has invited Lucy Grenning from Plant Services for this purpose. Sandy prepares a checklist to guide students during the interview. It consists of questions that the students had previously brainstormed. Sandy uses the checklist to interview Lucy during class time as a model.

5:2 Other Contexts
5:3 Classroom Performance

The next day, after careful planning and organization, she gives a 10-minute presentation model, narrating the story of Lucy, based on the interview from the previous day. She uses very formal language to model the respect that they should accord to their interviewees. She describes Lucy with visual aids, providing a physical description (a photograph), offering a brief description of her personality (a mind map), presenting a short summary of her life with a significant turning point (a timeline), and closing with a piece of advice from Lucy (a poster). Since she knows that the students will be evaluating each other, she also makes sure to use paralinguistic cues (e.g., eye contact) to demonstrate her connection with the audience. She distributes an evaluation rubric that will serve as the students' checklist and later her evaluation of them.

5:1 General Proficiency
5:2 Other Contexts
5:3 Classroom Performance

After the class discusses the model, Sandy shares the thank-you card that she sent to Ms. Grenning and tells the students to do the same after interviewing someone. Sandy suffered some embarrassing moments before learning that unscheduled visits to someone's office are not culturally accepted in the United States, so she stresses that students should make appointments before visiting people. Finally, Sandy reiterates how important this assignment is—to enhance the campus and local community's awareness of international students.

Sandy invites other ESL classes, her colleagues in the program, and some administrators to serve as an audience for the class biography presentations. The teachers arrange for the presentation to be active listening assignments, so the observing students are required to take notes. As students and administrators witness the success of the project and Sandy's contribution, their impressions about NNES teachers are tempered and Sandy unwittingly becomes an advocate for NNES teachers as a group.

5:4 Nonnative Advocate

Discussion

A. Study the vignette. List the varieties of English that Sandy is expected to use as a teacher in this program and when she uses them in the vignette.

[Answer Key A: formal and social: interviewing community members; persuasive: dealing with objections from the community and faculty members; formal: modeling for students; social informal: talking with colleagues; formal/informal, academic: working with students]

B. Discuss the following:

1. As an NNES teacher in an IEP in the United States, Sandy risks criticism from paying students (who are theoretically paying for the "native" experience) who resent having her teach them. How does she overcome this resistance? How does her nonnative English experience prove advantageous to her teaching?

2. How does Sandy demonstrate proficiency in social, academic, and professional English? Discuss which, if any, of these aspects of English is more important than the others and why.

C. What level of proficiency do you deem acceptable for NNES teachers? Consider pronunciation, grammar, and other expectations you would have if you were hiring teachers for an IEP program.

Vignette: English as a Foreign Language

Standard 5: Language Proficiency

Background

This vignette describes a university in Shenyang, China. In order to graduate, students need to pass a national English exam. All of the 30–40 students in each of the classes meet for four 50-minute periods of English each week. Usually there are separate books for listening and speaking, intensive reading, grammar, and extensive reading. Students seldom have the opportunity to communicate in English outside of class, so teachers typically use a tape recorder in listening and speaking classes to facilitate listening practice. Instructors of intensive reading explain the line-by-line meaning of texts, and translate if needed. Based on these texts, the students complete grammar exercises to prepare for quizzes on vocabulary and structures. Students are expected to do extensive reading on their own. Recent attempts to use more communicative activities have led to the development of new textbooks, but Bin Chang wants to try some additional teaching techniques. She has a solid reputation with the administration, faculty, and students, and she has been given permission to experiment.

Vignette

Bin Chang has been teaching at the university for 13 years. After attending several workshops on using communicative language teaching (CLT) in large classrooms, she is excited about trying some new oral communication activities. Until now, the administration has relied on native speakers to teach most of the oral communication classes, with the Chinese speakers focusing mostly on grammar and reading. Many of the Chinese instructors believe that native-English-speaking teachers are less equipped to teach grammar and writing, and that only native speakers should teach communicative skills. Bin's recent discussions with other NNES teachers outside of the university have led her to branch out in order to balance her teaching experience and to share discoveries with other instructors at her home institution. She becomes interested in teaching oral communication courses, proposes the idea to the administration, and is granted permission to teach a conversation class. Like most of her Chinese colleagues, she is enormously confident in her grammar teaching. However, native fluency is hard to achieve, and she wonders if her limited sociolinguistic competence will prevent authenticity in her presentation of situational English.

5:4 Nonnative Advocate

She is well aware of some of the pitfalls of using CLT in EFL contexts, so she is prepared to approach with caution. Teachers and students both resist new ideas; faculty members claim that CLT is difficult to implement in large classes, and students assert that communication is not relevant because the national exams are largely grammar based. Bin is especially sensitive that many of her colleagues disparage teachers who spend more time teaching communicative skills than analytical ones, because she knows that this is an artificial dichotomy that ignores the tremendous overlap between the two types of skills.

Although the administration frowns on team teaching because of the increased expense, she has found ways of collaborating on her own. Bin has befriended many of the international teachers, who have been good cultural resources and have shared interesting materials that she could adapt for her university-bound students. They often get together on the weekends, and they often discuss cultural differences. English is often the medium of communication, so Bin's social English improves rapidly. She has also been able to offer her English-speaking colleagues tips about Chinese culture and students. Because most of her international friends have been in the country for a while, their questions tend to be sophisticated and require thought on her part. They ask questions such as "How do students feel about cheating?" "Can it be negotiated?" "If so, what are the limits to its negotiation?" "Does student-centered teaching work in China?" "How about CLT?" and "How about the use of Chinese in the English language classroom?" Bin enjoys these topics, but feels frustrated discussing them in English because she is unable to articulate her ideas adequately. When she stops to consider this reaction, she realizes that these experiences of discomfort will help her empathize with her students, who are also often searching for the best way to express themselves.

After receiving permission to teach more oral skills, she decides to introduce some communicative activities slowly, making sure that they build on content the students have learned. She also receives permission to stray from the textbook, and with two other colleagues she plans an activity to discuss cultural norms and differences between the United States and China. She begins with a discussion about table manners. She prepares a one-page handout on a dinner scene from the film *Joy Luck Club*. Although the movie is somewhat dated, the themes are still relevant and, at the very least, will be an excellent example of how language register can lead to cultural clashes. The first part of her handout directs the students to watch a short clip and then answer some discussion questions in groups of four. After the students have discussed the questions thoroughly, Bin plays the video clip again, this time with captions so her students can check their responses. There is lively discussion when students compare responses, and Bin successfully models appropriate English as she leads the discussion.

Reflecting on the lesson afterward, Bin is especially happy about the development of her own communicative competence and believes that her varied opportunities to communicate in English have made her a better teacher.

Discussion

A. Study the vignette. List ways that Bin prepared herself to teach this communicative class.

[Answer Key A: 13 years of teaching experience, CLT workshop, discussions with colleagues]

B. Discuss the following:

1. In any institution, support from the administration is essential to change. How was Bin successful in convincing the administration to allow her to teach more communicatively? Discuss what she might have done had they declined her request.

2. What did Bin do to improve her communicative competence? Discuss other ways nonnative instructors might improve their communicative competence.

C. Bin benefits her institution by introducing her knowledge about CLT. What expertise could you share with your agency? How would you gain credibility with the other instructors and the administration?

Standard 6
Learning

Standard 6: Learning

Standard 6
Learning

*Teachers draw on their knowledge of language
and adult language learning to understand
the processes by which learners acquire a new
language in and out of classroom settings. They use
this knowledge to support adult language learning.*

The central focus of a teacher's work is understanding how people learn and, particularly, how people acquire language. Teaching, no matter how proficient, does not cause learning; rather, it enables, invites, and supports learning. There is no single or definitive view of learning, so teachers must

- know about theories of adult and social learning generally, and about second language acquisition in particular

- understand that these different styles of learning create varied ways of understanding, labeling, and interpreting what learners might expect from instruction and what they actually do

- recognize their own assumptions about learning and learners

- question what they believe about learning in the face of what is happening in their classrooms

- gather information from learners in the process of learning, analyze and interpret what they see, and rethink their approach, when necessary

Working to understand learning creates the ongoing dynamic through which teachers gauge and improve their teaching.

Standard 6: Learning Performance Indicators

6:1 Classroom Environment

- creates classroom contexts in which language acquisition can take place

- scaffolds language and content

- integrates instruction in oral language and literacy

- adjusts teacher talk to the English level of the learner

- provides language input, feedback, and opportunities for learners to use and extend English

6:2 Learner Activity

- provides learning experiences that promote autonomy and choice

- provides learning experiences that promote cooperation and collaboration

- creates classroom contexts in which learners can negotiate meaning through interactions with the teacher and with one another

- creates situations where meaningful messages are exchanged

- encourages learners to use their first language skills as a resource for learning English

- helps learners to develop metacognitive awareness and to use strategies for knowing about, reflecting on, and monitoring their own language

6:3 Learner Variables

- demonstrates understanding of the personal and contextual factors that affect language learning

- provides learning experiences that respond to differential rates and styles of learning

Vignette: Adult/Community

Standard 6: Learning

Background

This vignette describes the experience of Thomas McCarthy, an English as a second language (ESL) instructor in Illinois who teaches in an adult program. Several factors helped him understand the process of learning a new language: learning a foreign language in college, earning a certificate in teaching English to speakers of other languages (TESOL), and taking language acquisition classes and methodology courses. He teaches a high-beginning class, in which students are beginning to process the vocabulary they learned in the previous level in a more communicative way. The classes meet 4 days a week for 2 hours every class period. Students in this open-entry, open-exit program are very dedicated to learning if they feel they are making progress, but many have 40-hour-a-week jobs.

The curriculum requires Thomas to use a life-skill competency approach. The objectives for the course all relate to life skills, as does the standardized test the students take at the beginning and the end of the term. Early in his teaching career, Thomas taught several objectives at a time in a lesson at this level, believing that the more input, the better; he often said "give them as much as possible and something will stick." But as he reflected on student progress, observed other classes, and began to incorporate other assessment measures, he saw that students were not grasping as much as he expected. Thomas adjusted his teaching to thoroughly address one objective at a time in this lower level class.

Thomas is still not satisfied with his teaching. He is convinced that he can teach more effectively and become more sensitive to student needs, so he makes sure to stay abreast of new ideas and approaches. He attends workshops when possible and is active in the local, state, and international Teachers of English to Speakers of Other Languages (TESOL) conventions and conferences.

Vignette

Thomas feels confident in his abilities after 5 years of teaching. In this lesson, Thomas establishes the context by talking about his experience while in a restaurant the night before. He is very aware of the language he is using to talk to the students and does not slow his speech; however, he does use cognates when possible and opts not to use many long or complicated sentence structures. He recounts how good the food was and what he ordered. Then he asks the students to open their books to find the menu printed in the textbook. Students are asked in the practice portion of the lesson to take orders. They listen to a naturally paced recording with background noises and unfamiliar words, and write the information they hear on a handout that looks like a server tablet. The recording is at a natural pace.

Because of his experience learning another language, Thomas knows how easily students can become frustrated when too much information comes too fast. He finds it useful to teach students how to learn in addition to teaching course content. In this case, he wants them to learn

6:1 Classroom Environment

6:2 Learner Activity

that it is not necessary to understand every word. He communicates this by using a metaphor that will make sense to his students. In this case, he likens listening to seeing, explaining that if the students close their eyes, they cannot see anything. Encouraging them to keep their ears open to what is being said no matter how frustrated they feel, he explains that understanding one word (in this case a food item from a menu) represents progress. He then offers them strategies to use the information they hear to make educated guesses and to clarify what is being said.

Next, Thomas prepares the students to practice a dialogue in which they ask a partner "How much are the burgers?" "How much is the ice cream?" and so on. Although he has taught the singular and plural forms of the verb *to be* in various lessons, he reviews them because students who studied the structure in earlier lessons may not remember it. He explains to the students that learning grammar is a long process—and that they will acquire structures gradually and may even continue to make errors in structures they have already learned. Thomas used to become frustrated when students made errors in structures that they had mastered, but he now realizes that making mistakes is part of learning. He is also aware that many of his students had very little educational experience before arriving in the United States and that they might be slow learners; however, he continues to challenge his students to help them gain confidence in their abilities.

Thomas encourages his class to begin to think in English by using visuals throughout the lesson. He speaks only English in the classroom but sometimes addresses topics that are similar or different in English and the students' languages. He knows, for example, that some Asian languages do not have markers for the plural, so he alerts the Asian students that they might have trouble with the final "s" in plurals. The final consonants are deemphasized in some languages but are essential in English, so he explains to other students that they may have trouble pronouncing and hearing the ends of words.

Thomas understands that learning a language is a complex process, that some students need different or additional input because of their prior education and experience, and that not all students learn in the same way that he does. These realizations have helped Thomas become more flexible as a teacher and open to introducing different methods and strategies in the classroom. He is convinced, however, that meaningful context helps all students learn, because he has observed that people seem more apt to acquire structures and use language properly beyond the classroom when they have opportunities to apply what they have learned in meaningful situations. He offers students an opportunity in every lesson to apply the language they are learning in the classroom and encourages them to use it outside of the classroom as well. In this lesson, he asks students to develop their own menu in groups and to role-play taking orders. He then asks them to bring menus from the community to the next class meeting.

Many students performed as expected during the lesson, but five students did not participate in much except the dialogue and the application activity. Reflecting on how he might have set up the activity differently, Thomas realizes that his lesson had less group and pair work than his lessons typically do. He makes a mental note that these five students might learn more readily working in pairs than on their own. Thomas has become a keen observer of students, and he seeks out ways to reach each one through more effective teaching strategies.

6:2 Learner Activity

6:2 Learner Activity
6:3 Learner Variables

6:1 Classroom Environment

6:1 Classroom Environment
6:2 Learner Activity
6:3 Learner Variables

6:3 Learner Variables

Discussion

A. Study the vignette. Thomas demonstrates in the vignette that he recognizes many principles of effective language learning. Make a list of insights that make Thomas an effective teacher.

[Answer Key A: Answers may include: (1) He is aware of his own use of the language and how students may respond. (2) He realizes and imparts to the students that they do not have to understand every word they hear to understand the message. (3) He realizes and imparts to students that learning a grammar structure is not the same as acquiring it. (4) He alerts students that recognizing differences between their first language and English can help them learn. (5) He recognizes that students favor different learning styles, and he supports all these styles for learning a language.]

B. Discuss the following:

1. How did Thomas's knowledge of the students' first language help him teach more effectively?

2. Students, like new teachers, sometimes have misconceptions about what is expected of them. Discuss how students can misunderstand what is expected of them during grammar and listening activities. Then, discuss any other aspects of teacher or student expectations that can be confusing.

C. What strategies that Thomas implemented would help you learn a language? What other strategies might be most effective for you?

Vignette: Workplace

Standard 6: Learning

Background

This vignette describes an advanced writing program for an airline based in Asia. The program was designed to help customer service officers complete two tasks—to write promotional letters for upcoming events and special deals and to answer a range of written complaints by passengers.

During the needs-analysis and program-design stages, it became clear that the sponsors unrealistically expected that one course should suffice to teach all levels of learners. Furthermore, they wanted all participants to exit the program with the same high level of competency in English writing. Careful negotiation with the human resource manager and upper management led to an agreement that the provider would assess employees' levels of language proficiency and recommend the participants who could benefit most from the program. Of the 30 put forward for the training, only 13 had a high enough level of proficiency to benefit from the program. The participants selected were all graduates of Hong Kong universities and had been working for the airline for a minimum of 6 months.

Vignette

6:2 Learner Activity
6:3 Learner Variables

The instructor, Jocelyn Porter, starts the course by presenting the objectives and emphasizing that the participants will succeed only if they attend class and apply the new knowledge and skills in their work. Many of the learners have been making similar mistakes in their writing, so she explains how to eliminate these errors. She encourages students to take risks in their writing rather than cutting and pasting from flawed models, and she assures them that she will provide ample feedback so they feel encouraged to participate actively in the program.

6:1 Classroom Environment
6:2 Learner Activity

Jocelyn finds samples of good promotional writing and uses these in her lesson on complaint letters. She creates an authentic situation and clearly defines the context at the start of class. After dividing the class into groups of four, she asks students to read and discuss a model complaint letter and to speculate on the contextual variables of the letter (e.g., audience, content, purpose). In other words, was the complaint serious or trivial?

Jocelyn then distributes a model response letter, sometimes referred to as an *adjustment letter*, and has the students note the structural elements of the letter in the margins. The sections are

1. acknowledgment of the complaint

2. investigation of the complaint

3. outcomes of the investigation

4. resolution offer

5. final apology and closure

This becomes an outline on how to produce an adjustment letter. After the students have finished marking the sample letter in the margins, Jocelyn points out certain linguistic features in each section of the adjustment letter. For example, the investigation uses the past tense and often includes a short narration to reassure the customer that some action has taken place.

Finally, Jocelyn puts students in small groups and distributes a second complaint letter. She allocates 30 minutes for each group to draft a collaborative adjustment letter on a transparency or on paper that can be projected onto a screen. She encourages them to help, correct, and negotiate with each other at this stage. After they finish, the students correct and discuss their drafts. As she does at the end of every lesson, Jocelyn invites the class to apply their new knowledge in the workplace.

6:1 Classroom Environment

6:2 Learner Activity

Jocelyn uses the same approach for another lesson but varies it slightly to meet the needs of the students who did not quite master the first presentation. This time she decides to use scaffolding techniques, where students build on what they know. She starts with a discussion of complaints the learners have encountered in the past, based on which she creates a two-column table on the board. After putting all the complaints in the first column and the possible responses in the second, Jocelyn asks students to look for a pattern in the responses. When they identify the repetition of *would,* she writes on the board a structure that is at once direct, formal, and polite: "We would like to offer you . . ." She asks students to finish the sentence in various ways.

6:2 Learner Activity

6:3 Learner Variables

Now Jocelyn produces a new sample adjustment letter for the students to analyze. After they locate the formulation they have been discussing, Jocelyn asks the students in groups to identify similarly direct, formal, and polite structures in all sections of the letter. Finally, after much discussion, students are given another complaint and asked to produce another adjustment letter.

Jocelyn notes that, in this second attempt, some students who were struggling before have made some progress. She encourages them to continue working diligently and organizes the next lesson similarly, but now focuses on vocabulary so they can all continue to show marked improvement.

6:3 Learner Variables

Discussion

A. Study the vignette. Which of the performance indicators for Standard 7 is most clearly reflected in this vignette?

[Answer Key A: Every performance indicator was used. Learner activity is most apparent and includes promoting autonomy and choice, promoting cooperation and collaboration, fostering interaction, and creating situations where meaningful messages are exchanged.]

B. Discuss the following:

1. Discuss ways to use scaffolding to foster learning. How did Jocelyn do this? What could she have done differently?

2. What strategies, if any, did students learn to reflect on their own language in this lesson? How could Jocelyn have promoted this more?

C. In this vignette, Jocelyn recognizes that she must approach learners differently. Learning styles range from visual, kinesthetic/tactile, and auditory. How can all of these styles be addressed in a classroom setting? What would you have done to enhance these styles in Jocelyn's class? How might you address learning styles more in your own teaching?

Vignette: College/University

Standard 6: Learning

Background

This vignette takes place at a small community college in Utah. The main campus offers morning and evening classes, and the offsite location in a neighboring area offers evening classes. The ESL program includes four levels and serves slightly more than 200 students during each typical semester. The primary student population is Hispanic; however, a small number of international students from China, Japan, and Thailand also participate in the ESL program. The students hope to earn associate's degrees at the college or transfer to other universities in the state.

Ana Reynosa is the instructor of a low-intermediate writing class that meets in the morning at the main campus. Ana enjoys teaching writing to second language learners. She takes pleasure in learning about her students through their writing, and in witnessing the tangible progress in their expression across a semester. Her class this semester only has 15 students, 10 women and 5 men. Ana appreciates the small size, which allows for more individual feedback and conferencing with students about their writing. When studying for her master's degree, Ana taught at a large urban community college, where class sizes were nearly 30. Ana has been a part-time instructor at this college for 3 years.

Vignette

Ana meets with her writing class two times a week for 1 hour and 15 minutes. She plans carefully to make optimal use of the class periods that often seem to go by quickly. It is week 4 in a 16-week semester and she is beginning chapter 2 in her textbook. The theme of this chapter is *learning styles*. The main purpose is to teach the students a 3-step process for paragraph writing that they will use throughout the semester, and to have students focus on subject-verb agreement and present and past verb tenses. Ana begins by identifying and labeling the three steps: (1) gathering information, (2) focusing and organizing, and (3) writing, editing, and revising.

Step 1: In order to gather information about her students' learning styles, Ana guides the group through activities to help them think about how people learn. She starts by personalizing the lesson with an exercise that includes descriptive statements and prompts like this one:

6:1 Classroom Environment

6:2 Learner Activity

6:3 Learner Variables

"Some students choose to learn by doing. Describe a time when you learned how to do something by actually doing it." Observation statements followed by thought-provoking prompts such as these help the students to activate, clarify, and develop background knowledge. Next, Ana leads the students in some tasks that are more language specific. She provides sample student paragraphs about learning styles and uses them as an opportunity to introduce the concept of subject-verb agreement. She follows this with contextualized exercises that ask the students to select or fill in the appropriate singular or plural verb forms. Ana is raising consciousness in a strategic way before assigning a formal paragraph. To develop fluency, she has students do a 10-minute freewrite about a time when they learned something successfully. Freewriting does not penalize for errors, so it provides an opportunity for students to use new vocabulary and to try out ideas on paper without frustration or fear of making mistakes.

Step 2: Ana begins with instruction about topic sentences to move her students toward focusing and organizing. She explains the concept, and then uses a student writing sample to illustrate how, unlike in Romance and Asian languages, English writing tends to be direct and linear. She draws lines on the board to illustrate linear, circular, and back-and-forth development. She has students write sentences in their native languages on the board, and then translate the sentences word for word. The activity reminds students that word order within a sentence differs from language to language and allows Ana to demonstrate that the structure of arguments differs from language to language. Ana explains that one way is not better than another, but that it is important to satisfy reader expectations. English readers expect a topic sentence to guide them through a paragraph, for example, just as travelers defer to maps to find their route. The student writing sample does not have a clear topic sentence, so Ana underlines the ideas that provide control and direction for the paragraph. She asks the students to identify details in the paragraph and to suggest a topic sentence. Then Ana provides a list of sample topic sentences about learning styles, and has the students evaluate them and justify their responses.

> 6:1 Classroom Environment
> 6:2 Learner Activity

Next, Ana asks her students to look back at their own freewriting about a successful learning experience and analyze it in a similar manner, underlining the ideas that provide some control and direction for their thoughts. She then asks the students to use ideas generated during their freewriting to produce a topic sentence that includes two or three personal "best ways to learn." Their next focusing and organizing task is to identify two or three keywords or phrases in their freewrites so they can provide category labels for their best ways to learn, and then list supporting detail phrases for each category as a handout.

> 6:1 Classroom Environment

Finally, Ana works with her students on developing ideas for a concluding sentence, which might summarize, recommend, predict, or offer a solution. The students analyze concluding sentences from model paragraphs about learning techniques and identify which closing strategy each writer uses. Then the students draft a possible concluding sentence for the paragraph they will write.

Step 3: As she did with steps 1 and 2, Ana strategically incorporates guidance, student models, and opportunities for draft practice and peer interaction. After she explains academic format expectations for college-level writing, the students write their first drafts of a paragraph about personal learning styles, and edit for subject-verb agreement. During the next class, Ana explains the value of sensitive, constructive feedback from peers and facilitates peer reviews with a paragraph checklist handout, reviewing her main teaching points so far: effective topic sentences, keyword phrases and adequate details, good concluding sentences, academic format, and subject-verb agreement. Finally, the students write clean revised drafts to hand in to Ana for evaluation.

> 6:1 Classroom Environment
> 6:2 Learner Activity
> 6:3 Learner Variables

Discussion

A. Study the vignette. How does Ana create a classroom climate in which learning can take place? Describe three ways in which she applies her knowledge of second language acquisition and learning processes to her lessons.

[Answer Key A: Ana's strategies include the following: (1) She teaches that English speakers approach writing in a linear fashion. (2) She demonstrates questioning strategies by making observation statements followed by thought-provoking questions. (3) She describes linguistic differences between English and other languages (such as word order).]

B. Discuss the following:

1. Scaffolding is a teaching technique that allows students to build on what they know. Eventually the instructor removes the scaffolding so the learner can stand on his or her own. Discuss evidence of scaffolding in this vignette.

2. Ana planned a lesson on learning styles. How do different teaching styles reflect or legitimize different learning styles?

C. Identify one teaching strategy that Ana employs that would work for you, and another that would not. Which techniques have you chosen, and why? How would you teach differently in her setting?

Vignette: Intensive English

Standard 6: Learning

Background

This vignette describes a small intensive English program (IEP) whose emphasis is project-based learning. There are four levels in the program, each well coordinated with substantial integration of reading, writing, listening, and speaking. What makes this program distinctive is Communication Seminar (ComSem), a project-based language learning approach with an emphasis on communication skills necessary for interaction in an academic community. ComSem uses a series of activities that provide students with an opportunity to discuss and evaluate their performance. To begin, a student who has been designated as the class leader chooses a topic, divides the class into groups, and keeps time. Students participate in an activity called SmallTalk at the start of class, during which they work in groups and discuss issues. SmallTalk is followed by "mind mapping," where students synthesize their discussions in order to do the third activity known as "check-in." During check-in, group members report to the class on the content and nature of their discussions. Finally, the groups rate their conversations. Because of the complexity of this format, all instructors in the IEP are trained in this approach before teaching oral communication. The instructor's role is to observe and evaluate performance in order to identify areas of student need. In response, he or she produces vocabulary, pronunciation, and grammar worksheets, and teaches concepts based on individual or group needs.

The instructors at this IEP work in collaboration. Bill, Lynn, Polly, and Yuka are the four intermediate teachers for grammar, ComSem, reading, and writing. Lynn and Polly are the most experienced teachers. Bill is a recent graduate from a nearby TESOL program, and Yuka is a practicum student from the local university who is working with Polly. Bill teaches the oral communication course, and Polly and Lynn oversee his work to offer their expertise and advice.

Vignette

Although he has been trained, Bill is having trouble managing the ComSem approach. Bill assumed that SmallTalk should be an opportunity for students to relax, enjoy themselves, and chat about the weekend, but they have complained about the lack of feedback. Lynn and Polly work hard to convince him that learner-centered teaching does not mean a lack of planning, structure, or feedback. After visiting his class, they make some suggestions. They explain that during SmallTalk, Bill could help students make connections to the content of their reading class and he could help the leader generate more stimulating topics for discussion. For example, Polly, their reading teacher, describes a very lively discussion on friendship that students continued into lunch. At the next class, Bill overcorrects and gives feedback by interrupting conversations and correcting all grammar, pronunciation, and vocabulary errors. Lynn invites him to observe her class.

Bill is amazed by Lynn's class, in which an invisible structure appears to pull students together. Students organize the content of the instruction, the student leader assigns groups and

6:1 Classroom Environment

6:2 Learner Activity

6:2 Learner
Activity

keeps time, and the room is buzzing with activity. Students ask each other genuine questions rather than giving speeches, and two students in one corner of the room are actually arguing about global warming. Most impressive is Lynn's presence in the classroom. She is just as busy as the students. Without hovering meaninglessly, she floats quietly from group to group, busily recording grammar errors. She also takes note of when students occasionally code switch, or revert to their own language. Lynn knows that there are sometimes benefits to students using their first language and is intrigued by the influence of the first language on her students' English. Students enjoy learning about language acquisition theory, so Lynn decides that the use of students' first language to master English will be a good class discussion for a later date.

6:1 Classroom
Environment
6:2 Learner
Activity
6:3 Learner
Variables

Students in Lynn's class have become comfortable with the classroom environment she has set up, which includes an instructor who speaks minimally and distributes occasional worksheets. Yuka helps by also circulating through the room during discussion time and noting important tendencies; and by creating worksheets in consultation with Lynn. Furthermore, Yuka is Japanese, so she is able to offer Lynn insights about Japanese conversation styles and classroom participation. After 20 minutes, students synthesize their conversation by mind mapping, and two students disagree about the difference between ozone depletion and global warming. At check-in time, Lynn reminds them not just to report what individuals said, but also to work together on synthesizing their discussion around concepts. There is a stimulating energy as students prepare their check-in reports. Lynn and Yuka circulate from group to group. Because there has already been considerable coaching for this particular task, Lynn remains silent, taking notes and recording grammar errors. Finally, the students are ready to report on the conversation. Each group has selected a representative to give a summary of their conversations while the other students listen attentively. After the check-in, Lynn asks the groups to rate their conversation on balance, energy, and exchange, another technique with which they are very familiar.

6:1 Classroom
Environment
6:2 Learner
Activity

Although they rate themselves rather high, certain students acknowledge issues. One student claims that the Japanese girls in his group would not participate and were speaking Japanese to each other, leaving him and another student to speak to each other. Lynn decides to use this situation as a springboard for a cultural lesson and pursues the topic by asking whether the topic or something else prompted the Japanese students to participate so little during class. A discussion about cultural differences ensues.

Throughout the lesson, Lynn provides feedback in a very nonintrusive manner. She will follow up by producing worksheets that address problem areas that she identified while students were speaking.

Discussion

A. Study the vignette. List the steps in the ComSem approach.

[Answer Key A: (1) Class leader decides on topic, divides class into groups, keeps time; (2) groups discuss issues and topics, synthesize discussion, and evaluate activities; (3) instructor distributes worksheets based on student performance in group discussions; (4) instructor reflects on the effectiveness of the approach and how to improve.]

B. Discuss the following:

1. How is the classroom context created? Discuss the difference between Bill and Lynn's approach to establishing context.

2. Discuss the ways in which Lynn has created a genuine learner-centered classroom and the differentiated ways in which she provides rich sources of input, feedback, and opportunities for learners to use and extend English.

C. What conditions need to be met in order for the particular approach represented in this vignette to be successful? Could you integrate this approach in your classroom? Why or why not?

Vignette: English as a Foreign Language

Standard 6: Learning

Background

This vignette describes a well-established private language school in Kecskemet, Hungary. Classes typically have 20–25 students, more than at newer schools. Mike Westbrook was hired to teach some advanced conversation classes. Classes meet daily and usually last 50 minutes or an hour. Much of the work in this school is shift work, which means that he may teach as early as 7:30 in the morning and as late as 8:00 in the evening. Because he lives nearby, this suits Mike, and he uses the time between classes for preparation. Most of the students are middle class or affluent. Roughly half are university students enrolled in the language school as a compulsory part of their diploma, and the others are learning English in order to communicate with their non-Hungarian customers. Mike has recently earned an online TESOL certificate and is eager to try out some ideas.

He starts out excited about his new teaching situation. There is no textbook for his conversation courses. He has been asked to simply provide topics for the students. His Hungarian is fairly limited, so he is unsure of how to connect to his students and feels quickly as if he is losing their attention. He shares some newspaper clippings that his family has sent him from the United States, but the conversations are too unstructured and the students flounder. If Mike does not monitor the discussions, students speak Hungarian. He does not need to teach grammar, but finds this difficult because grammar is what he remembers best from his own secondary language courses. His students appear to like him fairly well, but he cannot tell how much they are learning. Two months into the session, he decides to ask them for feedback and is surprised to see the detailed list his class generates about how he can improve. One student writes: "English to us is an investment . . . we are not joking around here. This is our livelihood. It bothers me when the other students in class speak Hungarian."

Vignette

6:1 Classroom Environment

6:2 Learner Activity

Feeling a bit deflated because of the student feedback, Mike decides to teach more systematically. His students seem to love literature, especially as a way to debate and cajole each other, so he decides to use books to stimulate interesting discussions. His students are also keenly interested in world events, so he selects George Orwell's *Animal Farm* as a starting point. He knows that most of the students read and studied the work in Hungarian during high school, but convinces the administration that it would be worthwhile to buy the book for the students. He decides to incorporate literature circles into his course, a technique he learned in his training. He also uses several online resources for information about how to implement them. Literature circles rely on the instructor as a facilitator rather than an authority, so students can have real-life discussions on readings. In English as a foreign language (EFL) and ESL, the instructor usually chooses the text. Each student in a small group plays either a general role (leader, recorder, reporter, or timekeeper) or serves a more specific function like those that Mike establishes in his class.

When Mike introduces the project, he is careful to scaffold the instructions with a handout that clearly outlines the roles. The roles include illustrator, vocabulary keeper, summarizer, passage connector, and discussion leader. This first organized activity uses a short text so students can practice the new roles. Although Mike feels confident about the activity he has planned, he is unsure if students will speak English without monitoring. In each session, he allows one group to discuss the work in Hungarian as long as the members can report in English what they have discussed. As it turns out, the students are so excited about the content that they forget they are speaking English.

6:1 Classroom Environment
6:2 Learner Activity
6:3 Learner Variables

The literature circles prove to be an excellent catalyst for conversation topics. Often, Mike asks one member of each group, the passage connector, to write a quote on the board to offer students an opportunity to discuss how the text connects to their personal experiences. The quote might also serve as the discussion topic for the following class period. Mike knows that the literature circle needs to be well structured but varies the conversation routines to avoid boredom. Sometimes he prepares the questions on an index card, and the students move around the room. Other times, he organizes a simulated social party and has students float from student to student discussing the topics. While students are interacting with each other, Mike walks around with a clipboard noting relevant errors students are making in grammar, vocabulary, and pronunciation. After each session, he presents a mini-lesson on areas that require extra attention. He cannot prepare in advance for these mini-lessons, so they are only marginally successful at first. As the semester progresses and he becomes more proficient, however, he can even begin to predict where students will make their errors, and the mini-lessons improve markedly.

6:1 Classroom Environment
6:2 Learner Activity
6:3 Learner Variables

At the end of the unit, he has the class break into two teams. Each group works together, so every student is prepared to speak for 1 minute on a theme from the book they read, based on the topics that emerged in the conversations. If a student needs help during the presentation, someone else from the team can take over until a minute has passed. Then the second team presents a second theme, and they continue to rotate until all students have presented.

6:1 Classroom Environment

At the end of the unit, Mike redirects students' attention to the process they have just completed. Students have become so involved that they have not noticed the amount of English they have produced. Mike allows students to reflect and identify how the process has helped them learn English. Students realize that they not only sharpened their English skills but also had meaningful discussions and debates while doing so. Mike explains that the strategies they are developing can be used throughout their language learning experiences.

6:2 Learner Activity

Mike likes this approach because it meets the needs of students with various learning styles, but he recognizes that students will not all benefit to the same degree. He takes a few minutes to discuss learning styles with the students and expects to make adjustments throughout, in order to satisfy all student needs and learning styles.

6:3 Learner Variables

Discussion

A. Study the vignette. List the ways in which Mike promotes student ideas and encourages discussion and collaboration.

[Answer Key A: (1) Mike chooses a topic that interests students. (2) He assumes the role of facilitator. (3) He assigns a role to each student. (4) Students take part in topic choices for future lessons. (5) He initiates "social parties."]

B. Discuss the following:

1. What changes has Mike made in his teaching? Discuss how these modifications affect the outcome of the class. If Mike were to ask for feedback again, how do you think students would respond?

2. This vignette lists the roles students take in their groups, but it does not describe the students' responsibilities. Discuss the value of the different roles Mike has assigned and whether these roles will promote discussion and collaboration.

C. How do you help learners reflect on their learning? If you do not do so now, how could you incorporate this in your teaching? Does doing this help your students understand? If so, how?

Standard 7 Content

Standard 7: Content

Standard 7
Content

Teachers understand that language learning is most likely to occur when learners are trying to use the language for genuine communicative purposes. Teachers understand that the content of the language course is the language that learners need in order to discuss, listen to, read, and write about a subject or content area. Teachers design their lessons to help learners acquire the language they need to successfully communicate in the subject or content areas about which they want or need to learn.

Teachers understand that learners acquire language best by using it to fulfill real communicative needs, and not by memorizing rules, repeating meaningless drills, or learning lists of vocabulary. Adult English learners may be preparing for college, professional training, or the workplace, and they may be interested in learning how to adapt to their new communities and country. Teachers teach the language that learners need to develop communicative competence in these daily academic, work, and life settings.

Teachers help learners acquire communicative competence, which includes
*   grammatical competence, knowledge of the syntactic, phonological, morphological and lexical features of the language
*   discourse competence, the ability to understand the relationship between words, phrases, and sentences as an interconnected and meaningful whole
*   sociocultural competence, the understanding of the social rules of language use
*   strategic competence, the coping strategies used in unfamiliar situations or when grammatical, sociocultural, or discourse knowledge is incomplete

Teachers design lessons that help learners use language to learn about a subject and acquire communicative competence in that content area. Language is used to learn about content, rather than content being used just to practice language. Teachers design lessons that include real-world tasks and pedagogical tasks.

Real-world tasks might include
- practicing the oral interview for the citizenship exam
- comprehending a prompt for an academic essay assignment
- writing a résumé

Pedagogical tasks might include
- learning and practicing the *wh* questions that might be used in the oral interview
- understanding the vocabulary used in a writing prompt (describe, explain, etc.)
- learning the format of a résumé

Teachers may need to inform themselves about the language associated with the content areas that their students need or want to learn about. Teachers may use prior knowledge and expertise or acquire knowledge in the content area to develop a curriculum or plan lessons, or help learners develop strategies to learn on their own in libraries, online, or from others.

Standard 7: Content
Performance Indicators

7:1 Input and Practice

- provides a model of oral and written language in the content area

- provides input and practice in the different linguistic features of the language used in the content area

- provides input and practice in the discourse structures used in the content area

- provides input and practice in applying sociocultural rules that relate to the content area

- provides input and practice in coping strategies that can be used when grammatical, sociocultural, and discourse competency is not fully developed

7:2 Tasks in Content Area

- incorporates real-world tasks that give learners instruction and practice in doing activities specific to the content area in the four skill areas

- incorporates pedagogical tasks that give learners instruction and practice in using the language they need to successfully complete a real-world task

7:3 Content Knowledge in Lesson Planning

- uses prior knowledge or expertise in content area to develop lessons

- collaborates with content specialists to develop lessons

- teaches students investigative or research strategies to acquire content knowledge on their own

Vignette: Adult/Community

Standard 7: Content

Background

This vignette focuses on a low-intermediate class in a competency-based adult school in New York (United States). This particular class has 30 students from Cuba, Haiti, and Korea. The school has a complete curriculum that the instructors are required to follow. The school exists to prepare students for survival in the community and in college, if that is their goal. In this particular class, most students are hoping to get better jobs or to help their children in school, and a small number are considering college.

Leticia Albright decides what she will teach based on the school curriculum and student needs. Leticia is an experienced teacher who prepares her lessons carefully. She has learned that context and content are both important to successful language learning because they allow students to learn important skills and information that they can use in their lives while learning English. She has also found that students learn more when she builds on the context by providing content that is beyond isolated grammar rules and vocabulary.

Vignette

7:3 Content Knowledge in Lesson Planning

In the following lessons, Leticia teaches her students to read and write recipes as a significant part of a unit on food. She has chosen this objective because she knows that the students want to share the foods from their countries with the class. Leticia discusses the unit with a few friends who are knowledgeable about recipes. She is especially interested in basic recipes, so her friends offer her several that she analyzes carefully, taking note of the vocabulary and imperative verbs used.

Over the course of 2 weeks, students will not only learn to write recipes, but they will also work in teams to develop the class recipe book, type the recipes on a word-processing template, and make the recipes to share in a class presentation for school administrators.

7:1 Input and Practice

7:2 Tasks in Content Area

On the first day, Leticia explains the content of the project by establishing the context. She brings in brownies that she baked for all the students. After the students have sampled the brownies, she asks students to identify possible ingredients. She writes the students' ideas on the board and then passes out the recipe. As a class, they compare their predictions to the actual recipe. As a class, they discuss the parts of the recipe (e.g., servings, ingredients, instructions). In this lesson, the objective is to review quantities (e.g., cups, tablespoons, teaspoons) and related vocabulary.

7:1 Input and Practice

7:2 Tasks in Content Area

In the following lesson, Leticia reestablishes the context. She asks students in the warm-up to make a list of their favorite meals from their own countries. The class represents many nationalities, so she divides students into diverse groups of four or five. She will have students share their lists with their group and describe the food by ingredients and taste, but first she models the process by describing how she makes potato and vegetable soup and then asking students to write the ingredients and quantities they hear on a recipe template that she distributes. Leticia takes the opportunity to teach focused listening techniques. In order to be competent listeners, students need to develop strategies of filtering out unnecessary words and listening for specific information. Leticia encourages students to discuss what they have written about her recipe with their groups. They go over the recipe as a class, and Leticia rereads the recipe, asking students to make a list of every verb they hear and to notice the sentence structure. She explains that this will help them write instructions for their own recipe. She then reviews the imperative with a chart on the board and reminds students that this form is used for instructions on recipes and medicine bottles.

Next, Leticia begins to present new vocabulary (e.g., boil, peel, mix, beat, sift, drain). She passes out a sheet with three recipes. The recipes have instructions without verbs. She asks the groups to identify what the verbs might be and to complete the recipes. There are many possible answers and the groups struggle considerably to select the best answer. Because these are real recipes, students feel challenged to choose the right words. Leticia shares the actual recipes and tells students that in the next few classes they will develop a recipe book, and that these recipes and the brownies from the previous class will be her contribution.

> 7:1 Input and Practice
> 7:2 Tasks in Content Area

For the next lesson, Leticia brings in a cookbook from home and another one that her class created in the previous term. In another lesson, Leticia has students search for recipes on the Internet and share what they find. Leticia also shows them how they can search words on the Internet. In one of the lessons, Leticia teaches students clarification strategies and then asks them to go into the community to interview someone about his or her favorite recipe. She encourages them to formulate basic, simple questions to make themselves understood and to garner credibility with those they interview. She teaches them basic phrases so they are cordial and initiates a group discussion about what to expect culturally when approaching someone from the United States.

> 7:1 Input and Practice
> 7:2 Tasks in Content Area
> 7:3 Content Knowledge in Lesson Planning

In the next step of the process, the students write recipes in groups and then peer edit their work, print their recipes, discuss and describe their recipes, establish an organization for the book, write a preface, and send representatives to personally invite the administration to taste the recipes they have created. In the culminating activity, students share with school administrators their recipe book, the completed recipes, and short oral presentations about food from their countries.

Discussion

A. English as a second language (ESL) instructors must make sure they introduce a context that is meaningful to students, and there must be some real-life application. What is the context of the lessons in the vignette? List the ways that Leticia introduced and reintroduced the context.

[Answer Key A: Leticia brings brownies to class and has students taste them and predict ingredients; asks students to make a list of favorite meals; and gives students recipes to analyze and discuss.]

B. Discuss the following:

1. Discuss other ways that the context might have been established. The domain for Standard 7 is *content*. What is the difference between *content* and *context*? How are they both important?

2. Think of distinctive methods you have used or might use to establish the context of a lesson. Make a list of different ideas you have for establishing the context and presenting the content. Share your ideas with a group.

C. The vignette provides limited information about how Leticia develops the lesson on researching the Internet. Discuss how you might develop a lesson with this objective.

Vignette: Workplace

Standard 7: Content

Background

This vignette describes a program aimed at high-beginning speakers of English with only 3 years of secondary education. They are all employed in a retail chain in Asia that is owned by an English company. The employees were having difficulties communicating with coworkers and providing routine customer service at the retail shops, so the company owners contracted with an educational organization to provide an intensive comprehensive workplace communication program.

The company owners and the educational institution's staff worked together to establish performance standards for the participants of the program, and decided that there would be 12 units consisting of 3 hours of instruction per unit. During the needs-analysis process, the educational organization gathered materials that could later be developed for the courses. Each unit is based on authentic situations involving store procedures, and every lesson consists of simulated interactions between customers and coworkers relating to an area of customer service. The instruction uses words and phrases that are consistent with the types of customer service the owners deem appropriate for operational success.

Vignette

Oscar Martinez is very knowledgeable about the needs of the employees and the expectations of the company. After analyzing the data and surveys that were used in the needs assessment, he recognizes the need for clear direction and good instruction. He worked in retail sales before deciding to teach for the educational agency and feels very confident that he can help the employees.

> 7:3 Content Knowledge in Lesson Planning

Oscar reviews the objectives carefully and decides to do a lesson based on one of the objectives indicated by the company, dealing with customer refunds. He starts the class by asking students how many times they have purchased something they later had to return. He asks them additional questions about their experience making the returns such as how difficult it was and how cooperative the customer service personnel were.

After establishing the context and capturing the interest of the students, Oscar passes out a handout that he has prepared based on what he knows about the company. The handout includes a policy paper on returns that outlines most of the reasons for customer returns, along with 10 statements outlining the expectations of customer service representatives. Oscar discovers that the employees have not seen this information before; if they had, they would likely have had difficulties interpreting it. As a class, they go over the statements and discuss them in basic terms. As difficult words arise, Oscar writes new vocabulary on the board. Oscar then gives the class 15 minutes to complete the questions on the second page of the handout. They correct and discuss the answers as a class, and then Oscar tells the students to study the material for a test the next day on these or similar questions related to the company's return policy. He informs

> 7:1 Input and Practice
>
> 7:2 Tasks in Content Area

them that he will show their employer the results, to demonstrate student effort and progress and to justify the class.

7:1 Input and Practice

7:2 Tasks in Content Area

Next, Oscar passes out a form that customers are required to complete before being granted a refund. He writes on the board the information that goes on the form but does not tell students where the information belongs on the form. He allows students 5 minutes to complete the form and then asks a volunteer to complete the form on an overhead transparency.

7:1 Input and Practice

7:2 Tasks in Content Area

Oscar continues with the class by modeling a conversation. He has prepared a short authentic dialogue that students will practice for pronunciation and clarity of speech. The purpose of the dialogue is not to be a model to memorize, but rather a springboard to a role-play that students will do at the end of the class. When they discuss the return and practice the dialogue, inserting different reasons for returns and different responses based on the established policy, Oscar understands the company's concern about their employees' ability to interact with customers. Realizing the low level of the students' speaking ability, he understands that they may be unable to do the role-play at the end of class and decides to offer them additional mechanical practice of different situations at the next class meeting before they try the role-play.

7:2 Tasks in Content Area

At the next class, Oscar is happy to see that the students have prepared for the test on the policies and understand the concepts. Their efforts give Oscar hope that the dialogue practice will go well. After much review, they practice a new dialogue with more difficult situations. The students have gained some confidence and Oscar believes that they will be ready for the role-play. Students are not permitted to use any resources during the role-plays. He passes out 3 x 5 cards to half the students. The students with the cards are customers, and those without the cards are customer service representatives. Each card explains a unique customer service situation. Students with cards are asked to walk around the room, locate customer service representatives, and initiate role-plays. They must speak to five different students and perform a role-play with each. Oscar decides to see how much they really know by asking for volunteers to improvise with him in front of the class.

7:2 Tasks in Content Area

Oscar follows this same process to work on other objectives established by the company and indicated by the needs assessment. Students practice making initial contact, closing a sale, demonstrating product knowledge, dealing with disgruntled customers, and explaining credit. The process includes

1. establishing the context

2. practicing with a model or information from the company

3. taking an assessment

4. practicing with something from the customer's perspective

5. practicing a dialogue from a model

6. doing a role-play

Discussion

A. Oscar established the context early in the lesson. How did he introduce the context, and once the context was established, what specific activities did he set up to prepare students for the role-play?

[Answer Key A: He established the context by asking questions about returns. He prepared students by giving them models, vocabulary, opportunities to practice, examples, and models.]

B. Discuss the following:

1. Do you think it is important that the instructor be able to model company procedure and processes? Why or why not?

2. Think about Oscar's experience, and discuss what this suggests about assessments in a workplace setting. How might an instructor limit, learn from, and make use of such assessments?

C. This vignette is about a high-beginning class. If it were a more advanced class, how would you adjust the instruction?

Vignette: College/University

Standard 7: Content

Background

This vignette takes place at a small community college in an industrial section of a small New Jersey city. The college has one main campus, a small outreach center, and a new public safety academy. Five levels of ESL are offered at the main campus. There are nearly 700 ESL students, of whom 70% are Hispanic. The students represent 18 different countries and speak 10 languages. Most of the ESL students are immigrant residents; however, the program also serves a small number of international students on F-1 visas. The students intend to pursue associate's degrees offered by the college.

Michael Byrd is the instructor for the advanced reading class. This class is part of a learning community, in which the students take both an ESL reading class and a linked introductory psychology class. There are 22 students, 15 female and 7 male, in Michael's ESL reading class and the psychology class (plus an additional 11 students in the psychology class, which was also open for general enrollment). Most of the students in Michael's class are in their late 20s and are new college students; however, two men in the class are considerably older and had careers in their native Cuba, one as a minister and the other as a physical education instructor.

Vignette

Michael has been teaching at the college for only 2 years, but he taught English as a foreign language (EFL) in Japan for 10 years prior to accepting this position. While working there, he experimented with content-based approaches to ESL instruction. A year after joining the faculty at the New Jersey community college, he proposed a learning community section linked to the introductory psychology class, a required general education course for most associate's degree majors. Another faculty member successfully created an intermediate ESL learning community with an introductory computer science course, but this is the first time the ESL program has offered a learning community with psychology.

7:1 Input and Practice

Michael's first class meeting takes place the day before the psychology class. He is able to distribute both the psychology syllabus and his own. The psychology syllabus becomes the first authentic reading assignment, and it allows the ESL students to preview it before attending the first psychology class.

7:3 Content Knowledge in Lesson Planning

Michael decides to attend the psychology class with his students in order to better understand their experience. The psychology professor begins sitting among the students before class, talking with them as if he were another student waiting for the professor's arrival. Then, to their surprise, he heads to the front of the class and begins a lecture on perception. He speaks rapidly and includes many cultural references and much humor. The ESL students are rather quiet throughout this first class period, but their attention is rapt. The U.S. students that make up one third of the class are quicker to respond when the professor invites interaction. Michael thinks of many ways he can link his reading class to the psychology class.

Michael addresses the reading demands in the psychology course by having the students apply the reading strategies in the ESL textbook to the psychology material. For example, one of the first chapters describes a strategy called "textbook reconnaissance," which has readers rapidly preview every page in a book including the complete table of contents and appendices. Michael has the ESL students complete a textbook reconnaissance with their psychology books during one of his class periods. The ESL textbook also explains the concept of cultural references. Michael refers to examples about the 1960s that the professor mentioned during the first psychology class. He also asks students if they can define a "fun house," which is referred to in chapter 1 of their psychology book. In a section on perception, the book mentions looking in fun house mirrors. The only student who knows is a graduate from a local high school. With these two examples, the ESL students clearly understand what cultural references are, and why it is important to be aware of them when reading texts written for a U.S. audience. Michael asks the students to keep cultural reference lists throughout the semester, and he checks periodically to clarify them in the context of the psychology material.

> 7:1 Input and Practice
>
> 7:2 Tasks in Content Area

In addition to cultural reference lists, Michael works with vocabulary from the psychology class. He asks students to highlight new words and to keep a running list. He teaches students a variety of ways to learn new words and includes some of the selected words on his own tests. He also tests reading skills with selections from the psychology book, asking students to identify the main idea in a paragraph or to underline contextual clues to meaning in a sentence.

> 7:1 Input and Practice
>
> 7:2 Tasks in Content Area

Michael communicates with the psychology professor throughout the semester. He learns about his testing style, his reading expectations, and his research paper guidelines. The psychology professor's tests are multiple choice. Before the first psychology test, Michael spends time explaining multiple-choice test-taking strategies, and he emphasizes that doing well is as much about discovering the wrong answers as it is about finding the right answer. He encourages students to look at all the possible answers to check themselves, even if they feel sure they have already found the right one.

> 7:3 Content Knowledge in Lesson Planning

Michael is able to teach his learning community students very real lessons, and they appreciate his efforts. They complete the semester with credits earned toward graduation, and a great sense of confidence about how to be successful in their college classes.

Discussion

A. Study the vignette. Identify three ways in which Michael specifically provides language input, support, and practice with linguistic elements associated with psychology content.

[Answer Key A: He provides language input by using the textbook, discussing the psychology syllabus, and discussing the psychology class. He provides support by attending the psychology class; recognizing cultural items students may not know and discussing them; and helping students with test-taking strategies. He offers practice through the textbook and vocabulary activities.]

B. Discuss the following:

1. How does Michael take into consideration his students' needs when planning class?

2. Of the many activities Michael uses to teach his students in the learning community, which do you think is most valuable and why?

C. Establishing a learning community can present many logistical challenges but can also be quite worthwhile. What other college course might be effective to combine with an ESL class? How would you go about developing such a learning community?

Vignette: Intensive English

Standard 7: Content

Background

This vignette describes an intermediate ESL writing class in an intensive English program (IEP) at a private university in Freehaven, Oregon. Students from the Pacific Rim come to the IEP program to improve English skills and to prepare for entry to a university. Some plan to attend a university in their native country, and others will continue in the United States.

The program is project and task based, so colleagues collaborate on various projects that they will implement in their classes. There are usually two projects per session and four per academic year, and each one is content rich, integrates all skill areas, is student centered, and is highly structured with substantive teacher input. Ideally, the projects contain several layers of complexity, and the tasks encourage student collaboration, negotiation of meaning, and communication in the real world. The focus is on outcome, or what students can do after instruction, rather than what teachers have taught. Ongoing teacher and student feedback, as well as teacher evaluation, peer evaluation, and self-evaluation, enable the instructors to track student progress.

Miguel, Anna, Suzanne, and Jeff are the intermediate written and oral communication course instructors. They have collaborated on several projects over the years and have engaged their students in many meaningful activities. They have worked together to design the Downtown Landmark Project, and this is their second time implementing it. They learned a great deal from their first attempt and will incorporate new strategies to improve on the model that they have created.

Vignette

Reading: The first task that students must carry out with the help of their reading teacher, Miguel Suarez, is to choose a local landmark. In collaboration with the local chamber of commerce, Miguel has provided the students with brochures from area landmarks, including the clock tower, various parks, the opera house, the Imax theater, and the luxurious and recently renovated Dorport Hotel. After he distributes the brochures, he conducts a skimming and scanning activity to familiarize them with the landmarks. For homework, each student must write five questions about the landmark he or she has been assigned.

7:1 Input and Practice

7:2 Tasks in Content Area

7:3 Content Knowledge in Lesson Planning

Oral communication: Later that day, in their oral communication course, Anna Neddles conducts an information gap activity with city maps designed for tourists. The students are given destinations and roles. For example, "You are a shopkeeper at Jay Radley's novelty store and you are giving someone directions on the phone from River Park." In preparation for giving directions to the landmark they have been assigned, students practice giving and receiving directions without looking at their partner. They are then given a second set of landmarks in order to record their conversation for Anna, who will listen and provide feedback on grammar, pronunciation, and U.S.-appropriate listening skills. Based on the recordings, Anna teaches the

7:1 Input and Practice

7:2 Tasks in Content Area

students strategies for listening. For homework, students are sent into the community—to visit, photograph, and take detailed notes on their landmark.

7:1 Input and Practice

7:2 Tasks in Content Area

Writing: The next day, in her writing class, Suzanne Ostler provides a model for writing surveys about the landmarks, and students practice doing this in pairs. Over the next week, students are to speak to and survey six local native speakers regarding the landmarks they have been assigned. For example, Kumo wants to find out if locals know how long the clock tower has been in River Park and what its original function was. Ultimately, the students will act as tour guides for the rest of the class. Their final project will be to present brochures of the landmarks, by incorporating authentic items they have collected (photographs, key pieces of information, and results from their surveys). Students will be graded on their oral presentations for content (accurate information, description of the landmark, history, and other facts), organization (logical progression, clarity, and transitions), presentation skills (attention grabbers, volume, speed, eye contact, connection to audience, and use of note cards), and grammar.

7:1 Input and Practice

Students videotape their 5-minute presentations and listen to them alongside their notes so Suzanne can point out some differences between spoken and written English. In their oral communication class, for example, students are explicitly encouraged to use fillers, hedges, and circumlocution. In writing, Suzanne points out the need for clarity and conciseness. Suzanne is interested to see how their written language informs their oral production, and vice versa, and how their reading informs their writing. She presents a model description to the class, and they have also been reading about architectural design while working on their description of a building. She is impressed by the organization of their descriptions, and how the students structure their paragraphs about a landmark from the top of a building to the bottom or from the exterior to the interior.

7:1 Input and Practice

Grammar: After students give their presentations, they each write a five-paragraph descriptive essay describing their landmarks, which they give to the grammar teacher, Jeff, so that he can work with them on specific target structures. This week they are working on adjective clauses, so he pulls out all of the adjective clauses and creates various activities.

The Downtown Landmark Project is a success, and students have an opportunity to develop English skills as well as cultural competencies, coping skills, and knowledge about interesting landmarks that they will not soon forget. Each student's overall performance is used to evaluate his or her grade. The instructors have seen vast improvement from the first time they offered this project as an instructional tool and discuss how they might refine it even more for the next time.

Discussion

A. Study the vignette. What scaffolds do the teachers provide? Make a list and consider how this support shapes the context for their project.

[Answer Key A: Different scaffolding includes asking students to write out questions about authentic brochures, to practice giving directions before they are asked to provide directions to the landmarks, and to practice writing surveys before they are required to do it outside of class.]

B. Discuss the following:

1. What registers and varieties of English will students need in order to complete this project?

2. What are the end products? How might these products be used as content for future classes? How do you recycle student work?

C. How could one teacher accomplish the same outcomes in this project? Explain how you would set it up as the sole teacher.

Vignette: English as a Foreign Language

Standard 7: Content

Background

The setting for this vignette is a 2-year college in Kobe, Japan, where Jadi has been hired to teach conversation. Her teaching load is very demanding—four classes that meet three times a week. She is a native English speaker and taught at a few private language schools before landing this better-paying college job, so she is perceived to be an expert. But she is finding this new position more demanding than expected and does not feel qualified or adequately trained to do what she has been asked to do.

Vignette

Jadi's conversation classes do not seem to be going well. The textbook she has been asked to use, which is based mostly on grammar lessons and artificial dialogues, appears dated. There is very little presentation and she fears that the students do not find the book interesting. She supplements some of her lessons with tattered conversation books, but discovers quickly that both the content and her method are monotonous. The students are completely uninterested and sleep, self-groom, pretend not to understand, or actually do not understand. Her struggle to motivate students is palpable, and the administration offers little support. Despite her challenges, the students are her favorite aspect of the job.

7:3 Content Knowledge in Lesson Planning

Jadi prefers her students outside of class, however. They were not initially inclined to speak with her, but she comes to find them curious, lively, and full of questions. She decides to take advantage of these new friendships, and in the absence of a set curriculum, she feels that she has some flexibility in her lesson planning.

In addition to using the Internet to find teaching materials, she also begins to pay more attention to what her students are doing outside of class. The longer she lives in the culture, the better connected she becomes. She is learning Japanese (and finds it very difficult), so her students are the perfect authorities. Instead of insisting on English-only in class, she spends 10 minutes of every lesson with the students as her teachers on a particular grammar point, vocabulary item, or cultural issue. This seems to curb the problem of students speaking Japanese in class.

7:1 Input and Practice

7:2 Tasks in Content Area

Two days a week, she decides to experiment with conversation cards, a technique she heard about at a local teacher's conference. Students prepare a card in advance to use while engaging in a conversation. Students can create mind maps, draw pictures, or do anything that will serve as a memory aid while they are talking. Students must prepare their cards, and therefore their conversations, in advance. Jadi models some of the cards she found on the Web, many of which have elaborate, colorful displays.

One of Jadi's unstated goals is to have students collect these cards for future use. Because her contact time with the students is limited, she provides the conversation topics for the students. Knowing that they are interested in U.S. culture, she decides to prepare lessons based on five themes that they might find engaging: dating, sports, fashion, travel, and popular media. To promote lively conversation, she bases her lessons on readings for each topic and selects simple, authentic materials that are contemporary and appealing to this age group. For example, for the theme of dating, she selects two articles treating similar aspects of the topic, one from a U.S. teen magazine and the other from a Japanese magazine. She stresses that each article represents only one point of view and that neither can possibly reflect all U.S. or Japanese perspectives on the topic. When she has class time, she shares two or three wildly divergent views in order to spark controversy. For example, for the theme of sports, she brings in a story of Ichiro, a Japanese baseball player in the United States who is enormously popular in Japan. To provide an opposing view, she finds an article detailing the U.S. baseball players' exorbitant salaries and the player strikes of the day. Occasionally, she has to spend time adjusting the level of a reading for her students.

7:1 Input and Practice

Prior to each discussion, she provides students with some vocabulary, a grammar point, and one or two idiomatic expressions that pertain to the theme. If the topic is dating, for example, she teaches the conditional. She also teaches the students to organize their cards by identifying categories (personality, physical descriptions, actions). Finally, she introduces popular vocabulary and expressions (*babe, hottie, beauty is only skin deep*), again drawing students' attention to stereotypes. Students include the various grammar points and vocabulary items in their conversation cards and are expected to incorporate them in their discussions. Once the students are prepared, she allows them to converse independently and floats to ensure that everyone is using the introduced features and is speaking in English.

7:1 Input and Practice

At the end of their conversations, she collects and comments on the cards. Occasionally, she has groups of students perform for the rest of the class. She always tries to introduce one new simple activity by building on a previous lesson. For example, if students are having a hard time with a topic, she teaches them how to use fillers in English (e.g., *huh, hmmm, well*). Similarly, she presents circumlocution strategies and has students practice them by playing popular word games. On one occasion, she gives a mini-lesson on the importance of eye contact in U.S. culture.

7:1 Input and Practice

Discussion

A. Study the vignette. Identify the various ways in which Jadi "collected" content for her class.

[Answer Key A: from the students themselves, from the Internet, from U.S. magazines, from Japanese magazines]

B. Discuss the following:

1. In which ways is Jadi teaching sociocultural rules? What types of problems might she encounter? Cultural? Social? Institutional?

2. Jadi finds that using articles treating topics of interest with opposing points of view stimulates conversation. How did she discover what topics interested students? How else might she have tried to learn about student interests?

C. This class only minimally introduces authentic tasks. Outline how you might take the students beyond the conversation cards and incorporate more real-world application in the classroom.

Standard 8
Commitment and Professionalism

Standard 8: Commitment and Professionalism

Standard 8
Commitment and Professionalism

Teachers continue to develop their understanding of the relationships between second language teaching and learning through the community of English language teaching professionals, the broader teaching community, and the community at large. This knowledge, in turn, informs and changes both the teachers and the communities.

Teachers develop professionally by interacting with and reflecting on learning from the community of English as a second language (ESL) teaching professionals, the broader teaching and learning communities, and the community at large to help guide their teaching practices—planning, instructing, and assessing. Teachers also use an understanding of student learning gained from the classroom and the profession to inform and promote change in these communities. Teachers take the initiative to build relationships within these communities in order to support their own ongoing learning as teachers and in order to enhance the learning and well-being of their students. It is an ongoing and reciprocal process.

Teachers need to interact in the community of ESL teaching professionals to develop their own understanding and to share their teaching experiences. They also seek opportunities to interact with the broader educational community—to learn from and to inform other educators about the field of teaching English to speakers of other languages (TESOL), and to help other educators and trainers understand ESL learners and learning. Activities such as engaging in discussion with ESL colleagues and other faculty or professionals; attending and presenting at workshops and professional conferences; joining and actively participating in professional associations; and publishing in newsletters, magazines, and journals support this standard.

ESL teachers also build relationships within the community at large to learn from and inform the community about ESL learners and learning. Such relationships can be both informal and formal. Informal relationships may include participating in ethnic community events, attending safety meetings in a workplace, and meeting with families. Formal relationships may include serving on committees and writing articles for newspapers. As a result of these informal and formal relationships, ESL teachers learn about learner communities and use this knowledge to guide their practices. At the same time, they seek to inform the community about the nature of second language learners and their learning.

Standard 8: Commitment and Professionalism Performance Indicators

8:1 Gaining and Using Knowledge

- seeks out, interacts, and reflects on learning in teaching and learning communities and shares information with the teaching profession
- seeks out, interacts, and reflects on student learning and shares with teaching and learning communities
- seeks out, interacts, and reflects on knowledge about learners' communities and shares with teaching and learning communities
- pursues other opportunities to grow professionally

8:2 Skill Development

- is developing his or her professional voice
- is developing personal professional development plans
- continually develops his or her knowledge and skills to improve instructional practices
- balances professional responsibilities with personal needs

8:3 Advocating

- advocates for English language teachers and English adult learners in his or her teaching context
- builds relationships with the teaching and learning communities to support students' learning and well-being
- encourages social and political strength in learners and their communities
- serves as a professional resource in all learning and teaching communities

Vignette: Adult/Community

Standard 8: Commitment and Professionalism

Background

Curtis Shale is a full-time instructor at an adult school in Texas. After 10 years of part-time teaching, he recently completed his master's degree in TESOL. He has taught many levels and courses at the school and currently teaches two high-beginning classes. He is a good teacher who works closely with the other instructors and, since learning from his practicum to look critically at his teaching, he is always seeking new ideas, books, and approaches.

The school is relatively large. Its 2,300 students are mostly Hispanic and almost entirely from Mexico. The 20 full-time faculty members mentor the 75 part-time faculty members and often interact positively with them. The full-timers also frequently engage in professional service in addition to their teaching.

Vignette

Curtis was very active during his master's TESOL program. He was instrumental in assembling a group of teachers to study for the comprehensive exams. He organized all the notes taken by 15 teachers. The group pooled their resources and produced a comprehensive study guide that helped them prepare for an all-day essay test on various and detailed subjects. This professional experience prepared him for leadership experiences in his career. | 8:1 Gaining and Using Knowledge

Now Curtis has noticed some disturbing trends in one of his high-beginning classes. The school does not offer a literacy-level class, so students start at a low-beginning level. Some students have high school diplomas and a select few are university graduates, but the average student has attended only about 6 years of school in his or her home country. When students with little education are placed in his high-beginning classes, the disparity of education in the group makes it hard for him to satisfy everyone's needs. Students with limited education begin to drop out of his classes. | 8:1 Gaining and Using Knowledge

He recognizes that these students need institutional support and suggests that the ESL committee address the issue. The department members, who are involved in many other projects, dismiss his concerns because there are too few literacy students to warrant a new class. After several months, however, Curtis decides to take on the cause himself. He begins researching literacy issues in ESL, attends the annual international and regional Teachers of English to Speakers of Other Languages, Inc. (TESOL), conventions, begins to discuss ideas with part- and full-time colleagues, researches articles online, and even joins a blog on related topics. When he finds the blog unsatisfactory, he starts his own. The blog, although not wildly popular, attracts a handful of other instructors with similar concerns. | 8:2 Skill Development

Curtis meets with the ESL committee again and this time presents a plan to identify literacy students through demographic information provided by the state standardized test data that the school collects. He suggests a calling campaign to survey and approach the at-risk students. He also wants to meet with the school outreach program to propose an approach to reaching these | 8:2 Skill Development students. The department is impressed and gives him the green light to proceed. He is surprised but delighted that several full- and part-time teachers agree to participate in a subcommittee to work out the details.

While meeting with the subcommittee, Curtis discovers that not only do they need to find students to attend a literacy course, but they also need to produce a curriculum. Curtis shares the research collected by the subcommittee with the ESL committee and suggests that they request money from the administration to hire a consultant who can advise them as they plan a course. The subcommittee is given permission to hire a consultant and to schedule several meetings with her during project development. This proves extremely beneficial to the curriculum, and it also gives Curtis a voice in professional development that he has not had before. He now has a positive contact with a well-known expert in the field who sees Curtis as an asset to the profession. It is not long before Curtis is contacted by other experienced people in the field and becomes directly involved in research and practice.

With his success in developing a literacy curriculum, Curtis gains the confidence to volunteer in a mentoring program that his school has established; experienced teachers volunteer to observe a volunteer mentee. After the observation, Curtis discusses his reactions with the teacher, and together they decide on a technique that would be productive for him or her to try. Then Curtis invites the teacher to observe his class so he can demonstrate the technique. After another meeting, Curtis does a final observation of the mentee's class, and they have a final conference. Curtis enjoys this process. He loves interacting with experienced and new teachers, because he enjoys learning new strategies and refining his teaching philosophy.

Curtis continues to pursue the literacy issues that first interested him. He attends statewide TESOL conferences and coordinates with others from his school who might also attend. He downloads the program booklet and makes a schedule of workshops and presentations that will be most productive for him. When he returns to work, he shares ideas with his colleagues and submits articles to the school's quarterly teacher newsletter. He tries most of the new ideas in the classroom. Some work immediately and he incorporates these into his instruction. Those that work less well motivate him to improve his teaching. He is contemplating giving a presentation at one of the larger conventions. He thinks he might submit a proposal if he can find someone who would be willing to work with him.

Curtis has presented on various occasions at local conferences and at his school. He believes strongly in students and hopes that his contributions might improve the teaching of other enthusiastic professionals. At the last conference, he invited one of his mentees to present with him. The mentee learned that she also had experiences to share and is now strongly considering presenting on her own. Curtis advocates for the professional development of all employees, and encourages the administration to fund as many teachers as possible to participate in local conferences.

Discussion

A. Study the vignette. Curtis believes in professional development. Identify several ways that the vignette demonstrates this fact.

[Answer Key A: His desire to grow professionally stems from a concern for meeting student needs; he volunteers to do mentoring and write articles for the teacher newsletter; and he demonstrates that he enjoys learning new strategies.]

B. Discuss the following:

1. At Curtis's school there is a set system for mentoring. However, mentoring can take many forms. Discuss other ways that mentoring might be implemented.

2. What benefits might there be to presenting ideas at a convention, conference, or for other instructors? How can presenting one's work help to develop the skills suggested in the performance indicators for this standard?

C. Curtis might have become discouraged when no colleague in the committee initially shared his concern about the need for literacy classes. What motivated him to continue? What would motivate you to continue? Explain how you might have proceeded.

Vignette: Workplace

Standard 8: Commitment and Professionalism

Background

Teaching ESL in a school setting is very different from working as an English trainer in a workplace setting. One main difference is that the workplace trainer has as his or her boss both the company that hires the school and the school itself. Educational organizations assess the holistic needs of students, whereas companies consider only the trainees' work-related learning needs and often have expectations that exceed realistic outcomes.

Instructors in workplace settings often work without the support of colleagues and the curriculum direction that is typically present in a school setting. Workplace trainers need to develop professionally and feel committed to what they are doing, but they are often responsible for doing so on their own.

This vignette looks at one trainer, Peter, and how his experience as a workplace trainer helps him develop new skills, enhances his commitment to ESL training, and energizes his professionalism.

Vignette

Peter is assigned to work at a workplace setting by the community college that employs him. He begins his first workplace assignments feeling confident about his knowledge and skills as a community college ESL teacher, but uncertain whether these skills will be appropriate in a workplace setting.

His first few teaching assignments in the workplace did not go as well as he expected. Before developing a curriculum, he performed a needs analysis on the trainees that he was hired to teach. He prepared generic training materials. Yet, one complaint from the companies where he provided training services remained constant. His curricula did not meet the specific needs of the company paying for the training.

8:1 Gaining and Using Knowledge

Based on these negative results, Peter starts analyzing how to better meet the needs of the paying customer. The first needs assessment Peter conducts identifies the students' language proficiency specifically in reading and writing, but does not target workplace tasks. In an effort to identify the trainees' required language level and the skills needed for their jobs, Peter develops a survey that is intended to clarify student needs in these areas. He also realizes the importance of communicating with the supervisors and fellow employees of the hiring company. By doing so, he learns whether or not they detect progress, and he inquires about new problem areas. The information he gathers will help him improve his training and thus the company's view of the project.

Peter realizes that he needs to change his approach when designing workplace programs. He also realizes that training materials have to address the needs of the paying customer. Reflection on his teaching leads him to conclude that his old ESL college approaches are not very effective in this context. He starts to read about workplace training in general and discovers that it is important to involve all the stakeholders in both the curriculum design and the evaluation process. It is also important to be able to develop materials from authentic sources that are tailored to the particular audience. Peter changes many of his ideas on needs analysis, curriculum design, and methodological approaches for workplace settings.

Although this period of adjustment is challenging, Peter believes that he needs to develop a different style of commitment and professionalism for his new job as an ESL workplace trainer. He spends more time in the workplace and involves key workplace stakeholders in ESL training decisions.

In the workplace context where Peter is now working, his employers must continue to view him as an expert if he wishes to have his contracts renewed. Working on his own in a new context means he has to redefine himself as an ESL trainer. This new role forces him to develop professionally in three important ways:

1. Peter has to accept that a generic ESL syllabus will not meet the needs of the highly specific requirements of a workplace. This does not mean that Peter's expertise developed for an educational setting is not relevant, but that he needs to build on his previous experiences by acquiring new knowledge and skills related specifically to workplace environments.

2. Peter needs to spend much more time familiarizing himself with the context of the job and the people in the workplace to identify the gaps in job performance in the workplace. This means becoming comfortable with a new community of colleagues.

3. Peter needs to change his role in this new context as a workplace trainer. No longer is his role confined to the delivery of a preset syllabus in the classroom.

Peter becomes a language consultant in the workplace. As his professionalism and commitment develop, he becomes a reliable resource for the workplace when other communication problems in English arise. For example, supervisors begin to ask Peter to edit senior management reports, and the personnel department asks Peter to design a language screening test for recruiters and potential supervisors. They also ask for Peter's input on the language aspects of their quality assurance processes.

Not only does Peter develop a new perspective on his work as an ESL trainer, but he also contributes significantly to the company and becomes a key professional resource for this workplace.

8:1 Gaining and Using Knowledge

8:2 Skill Development

8:3 Advocating

Discussion

A. Study the vignette. Peter has a distinctive challenge because he is largely isolated from other teachers. List his interactions and how they affect professional development and professionalism in general.

[Answer Key A: Peter sees that he has to redefine his role and build professional relationships with the stakeholders. He tries to understand the inner workings of the company as a resource for developing his lessons.]

B. Discuss the following:

1. Discuss ways in which Peter continually develops his knowledge and skills to improve his instructional practices.

2. Peter becomes an asset to the company, and yet he is still employed by the college. How might he justify his extra work for the company? What might he do to balance his professional responsibilities and his desire to improve professionally with his personal needs?

C. The vignette characterizes Peter's isolation from other instructors and development of professional relationships in the company, but doesn't suggest how Peter could interact more broadly with other teachers. What would you do to continue building relationships with fellow instructors and to stay current with teaching strategies and approaches?

Vignette: College/University

Standard 8: Commitment and Professionalism

Background

John Carleton has been a full-time instructor at a large public university in the Midwest for 3 years. The ESL program at the school offers four undergraduate classes and three graduate-level classes, and John has taught most of the classes in the program. He generally has two preparations for the four classes he teaches each semester. The coursework in his master's program (at the same university) included a fair amount of reflective writing about classes that he observed or taught and required extensive interaction with his peers, and he continues to be thoughtful about his teaching and to work collaboratively. His master's program also instilled in him the importance of ongoing professional activity and research.

Vignette

John spends the first 2 years of teaching familiarizing himself with the program and course goals, curriculum content, and student population. During this time, he continually improves his teaching by

- meeting regularly with his colleagues to discuss course goals and materials and to norm himself on grading standards

- developing and using student information forms to learn about his students' ethnicity, educational experience and goals, and interests

- using writing conferences to further individualize instruction

- maintaining a log in each class, to note the successes and weaknesses of instructional activities and to use this information to discuss his teaching with his colleagues and to plan subsequent class sessions and courses

- studying end-of-semester evaluations of his teaching, and discussing the results with his coordinator to get validation for things done well and suggestions for improvement

> 8:1 Gaining and Using Knowledge
> 8:2 Skill Development
> 8:3 Advocating

During his second year, he resumes research on a topic he had studied extensively in graduate school, corpus-based research (the study of collections of words or the lexicon in various environments). This work allows him to develop new materials relating to patterns and lexical choices for reported speech that his colleagues and students eagerly welcome.

> 8:1 Gaining and Using Knowledge

After 2 years of teaching, John feels fairly confident teaching the integrated skills courses and the composition courses, but he remains concerned about his performance in a course he has taught only once, a graduate-level oral skills class for students serving as international teaching assistants (ITAs). This is an area of teaching and a student population for which his master's work and prior teaching in Thailand offered little exposure. After teaching the class the first time, he talks at length with his colleagues who also teach the course and joins a professional online discussion group focused on teaching ITAs. He prepares to teach this class again by doing

> 8:1 Gaining and Using Knowledge
> 8:2 Skill Development
> 8:3 Advocating

extensive reading on training ITAs and by learning more about the 2-week intensive training sessions for ITAs that his university offers each summer.

8:2 Skill Development

The second time he teaches this graduate-level course, he incorporates some of the techniques he learned in his graduate program. He has the students write reflective journals about their experiences and difficulties as teaching assistants, and he follows up with small-group and whole-class discussions about potential solutions. This process allows him to incorporate learner input in his course and to address student concerns about the pragmatic and linguistic aspects of their interactions with the undergraduate students they teach and the professors who teach them.

8:2 Skill Development
8:3 Advocating

After further discussion with colleagues who have also taught this course and with his program coordinator, John decides to undertake a long-term project with one of his colleagues to determine the current needs and concerns of departments at the university who employ a large number of ITAs. He will begin by designing surveys to get more data about the departmental expectations of ITAs and their concerns about performance. He is excited that this work with his colleague and the campus community will enable him to gather information in order to advocate for learners and their professors. His long-term plans are still somewhat vague, but he hopes eventually to organize workshops for undergraduates, professors, ITAs, and colleagues from his own program. He will work with his colleagues, his coordinator, and the ITA training program at every step of the process.

8:3 Advocating

John regularly attends regional TESOL conferences and goes to national TESOL conventions nearly every year (based on his school's ability to fund him). At the conferences, he focuses on ITA issues and the teaching of composition, which is the subject of most of his classes. He has recently submitted proposals to regional conferences on his reported speech materials and his ITA work. He hopes soon to publish his work in state professional newsletters.

8:2 Skill Development
8:3 Advocating

As John approaches the end of his third year of teaching, he feels quite confident about his composition courses and has decided to become involved in a materials-writing project that he learned about from his coordinator. It includes a series of academic writing textbooks by a major publisher of English as a foreign or second language (EFL/ESL). Having always been interested in materials writing, he investigates and eventually signs a contract to write one of the textbooks. When he signs on, he realizes that the publisher is imposing a formula on these texts that will prevent him from being as creative as he would like; he decides that involvement in the project will teach him about the publishing world in general, and the textbook-writing process in particular, so he will be better prepared to write textbooks more autonomously in the future. Thus far, he has found the work interesting and challenging, and he is looking forward to devoting his full attention to the task during summer break.

Discussion

A. Study the vignette. John's master's program helped him become a reflective, collaborative teacher interested in professional development and advocacy. List ways he has demonstrated this in his first 3 years of teaching.

[Answer Key A: He maintains a reflective log, he reviews his end-of-year evaluation, he speaks to colleagues about approaches and joins an online forum, and he does a project with a colleague.]

B. Discuss the following:

1. How does John gain knowledge about his teaching and course activities? Discuss the effectiveness and limitations of these techniques, and propose other methods that you might wish to use.

2. John plans to bring together diverse communities in his university (undergraduates, ITAs, ITA trainers, professors from other departments, colleagues from his department) to enhance the effectiveness of his ITA students. Discuss how this project relates to the performance indicators.

C. In addition to his classroom-related activities, John is pursuing other opportunities to grow professionally, such as writing a textbook for publication. What professional interests would you like to pursue that may or may not directly relate to your classroom teaching? How, specifically, could you explore these, and how might doing so influence your teaching?

Vignette: Intensive English

Standard 8: Commitment and Professionalism

Background

This vignette describes an instructor's professional efforts at an intensive English program (IEP) in the United States. The program offers four well-coordinated levels, from beginning to advanced intermediate, and the project-based courses integrate reading, writing, communication, and grammar. The IEP is connected to a private university to which students travel from all over the world, including Colombia, Japan, Korea, mainland China, Mexico, Taiwan, and Venezuela. Many of the students are in the United States to pursue either a bachelor's or master's degree. As is typical in intensive programs, students arrive with high expectations, have some traditional ideas about learning, and are usually prepared to work hard.

Vignette

Jennifer is a new teacher at this IEP. She feels fortunate to have this position because she was chosen from a pool of 50 qualified candidates, all with master's degrees. She attributes her hire largely to one especially well-formulated response during the interview. When asked about pet projects or research that she would be interested in pursuing, she described several in detail. She knew from her networking experience in graduate school that a position requiring a master's degree would require more than teaching.

8:1 Gaining and Using Knowledge

8:2 Skill Development

She was the newsletter editor for a marketing letter distributed to current students, alumni, the university community, and other interested parties during her TESOL master's work, so one of her first extracurricular duties in her new position is to create and edit an online ESL student newsletter that will feature student activities, achievements, and other newsworthy stories. Although the program has a way of tracking students, the program has made little effort to stay in contact with alumni. Jennifer's position depends on incoming students, and ESL enrollments are notoriously uneven, so she is eager to recruit and retain students. She believes that alumni contact is a good place to begin.

8:1 Gaining and Using Knowledge

8:2 Skill Development

At the IEP, each of the new teachers is paired with a mentor teacher. In addition to observing the other teacher's classes, the mentor teacher helps the novice teacher set up a teacher research project. Jennifer knows that planning for three classes can be very time consuming and is initially a little hesitant to pursue this additional work, but she quickly understands that she can integrate the data collection in her lessons. After one semester of collecting data from her upper-level writing course, she spends some of her break analyzing the information. Having recently attended a training workshop on outcomes-based assessment, she is especially interested to find out if students actually learned what she taught them. In addition to reviewing standard English rhetorical patterns with the students (expository, narrative, descriptive), she occasionally deviates from the curriculum to introduce other written genres. Her favorite among them is West African poetry.

Most of Jennifer's students appear to be unfamiliar with African literature, so she is especially interested in collecting data on their perceptions of these poems before and after reading. As a continuation of her master's research, she is also curious to learn what they know about colonization. In order to introduce students to the concept of postcolonization in Africa, she begins by building on what they know about their own countries. From past experience, however, she suspects that students do not know about the indigenous populations of their native countries. She decides to keep this pilot project fairly simple. After introducing the topic, she begins with two journal questions: "What does colonization mean to you?" and "Is there evidence of colonization in your own country?" She collects their responses and makes copies so she can contrast this with her second data source: recordings (with student permission) of small-group discussions about three West African poems that the class has read and discussed.

As she predicts, the students' reactions are mixed; some speak of liberation versus oppression, and others do not understand the topics. Using their confusion as a critique of her teaching, she decides to be more deliberate and less rushed the next time she teaches poetry—to introduce the genre, provide a greater range of poetry from different countries, contextualize the poets and their work, and help students with the themes. She also decides to collaborate with the reading teacher, who has tired of some ESL texts that she has been using. Midway through the semester, these two instructors submit a proposal outlining the project to their regional conference and at the meeting of the international organization, TESOL. Having been encouraged to present her work and publish while a master's candidate, Jennifer is accustomed to doing this type of work.

> 8:1 Gaining and Using Knowledge
>
> 8:3 Advocating

Full-time faculty members are also expected to serve on at least one university-wide committee. As a new faculty member who represents international students in a post-9/11 environment (September 11, 2001, was the date of a terrorist attack on the United States, in which the Pentagon was attacked and the World Trade Towers were destroyed), she volunteers for the social justice committee. One of her major concerns is the lack of diversity on campus, and she wonders if there is a way to start a conversation partner program between the native-English-speaking students and the ESL students. Because the university's modern language department offers Spanish, and many of her students are Spanish speakers, she writes a proposal to the chair that is received favorably. The communications department and the School of Education have also expressed an interest in participating. With her colleagues, she works to establish a way for both the ESL students and the undergraduates to earn credit for enrolling in a conversation partner program.

Discussion

A. List ways in which Jennifer has developed her professional voice.

   [Answer Key A: Answers include: (1) She developed her professional voice by creating a school newsletter. (2) She presented her work at conferences. (3) She participated in committee work.]

B. Discuss the following:

   1. Study the vignette. How will Jennifer's teacher research project assist her in learning more about her students and her own teaching?

   2. ESL teachers often do much more than teach. What extra work does Jennifer take on? Has she taken on too much? How can she avoid early burnout?

C. What steps could you take to incorporate teacher or action research in your own classroom?

Vignette: English as a Foreign Language

Standard 8: Commitment and Professionalism

Background

This vignette describes an English class at a university in Oaxaca, Mexico. With more than a million English-speaking residents in the city from all over the world, many people are seeking employment as English teachers. Teachers are hired at the many private language schools or at the university, where jobs pay better. English classes at the university meet only three times a week and range in size from 30 to 60 students. The long-term instructors have been complaining that students resist academic reading and lack the study skills necessary for sustained academic work. Ezme O'Brien has been hired to teach three advanced reading courses. She is expected to integrate some written and oral communication into her class, but her main charge is to improve student reading skills in both English and Spanish.

Vignette

With the exception of some field experiences and a practicum for her master's degree, this is Ezme O'Brien's first teaching experience. Until recently, she has found many aspects of the job very challenging, and on several occasions she has wanted to return to the United States. She has been asked to teach English content-based courses that she finds daunting. Although she is familiar with the educational theory of English teaching and quickly gets feedback that students' reading in all subject areas has improved as a result of her course, she is not knowledgeable about U.S. history or western philosophy.

To make matters worse for Ezme, English language instruction at the university is not a priority, and many students take English only as a prerequisite for graduation. Her predecessors earned a reputation for incompetence and lack of professionalism, so Ezme and her fellow English teachers do not feel accepted by their Mexican colleagues. In one of her classes, some of her students have been very outspoken about U.S. corporate and military presence in third world countries. A politically active person herself, Ezme tries unsuccessfully to work this tension into her lessons. Although she has seen other teachers facilitate very animated discussions, she does not know how to prevent the more "radical" students from dominating discussions while the more reticent students sit on the sidelines feeling bored. She decides to take two steps to improve her courses—to focus on what she does well (teaching reading strategies) and to solicit help from a colleague in the ethics department. Hector, a native Mexican who is also a recent hire at the university, has become a popular instructor. When Ezme asks why, her students tell her that he connects with them.

At first, Hector and Ezme chat informally before and after faculty meetings or in passing on campus. Eventually, Ezme suggests that they observe each other's classes; this was an established practice at her graduate institution. Hector thinks that he lectures too often and relies too heavily on his acting skills to entertain his students; he is eager to improve his teaching and loves the idea. She suggests that his content should drive his method and offers some creative outcomes-based assessment ideas. She also encourages him to opt for debates or panel discussions rather

8:1 Gaining and Using Knowledge

8:1 Gaining and Using Knowledge
8:2 Skill Development

than lecturing on topics that lend themselves to point-counterpoint. Whereas she can offer pedagogical strategies, Hector offers content ideas. He knows, for example, that students really enjoy the history of Mexican colonization and its effects on contemporary Mexican language and culture. Ezme also sees how Hector keeps the more dominant students in check during class discussions by encouraging them to ask questions and lead discussions. He teaches them to do this objectively, so they learn to ask questions and to keep discussions going, and only to share their personal views at the end.

| 8:3 Advocating |

Both Ezme and Hector decide to introduce a few literary genres in order to present multiple postcolonial perspectives. Hector finds articles in Spanish from Mexican sources, and Ezme locates articles on similar topics in English from U.S. sources. They intentionally build tension into their lessons. They share many of the same students, so Ezme and Hector are able to compare notes. The students report that they thought they might resent the U.S. perspectives or find the topics repetitive or boring because both teachers were discussing similar topics, but they come to see concrete evidence for the fluid nature of language and its relationship to power. Ezme notices that the students become more motivated and responsive to her suggestions on improving their study skills. She attributes this success to their new interest in the class.

| 8:1 Gaining and Using Knowledge |

The constructive input from Hector is Ezme's greatest teaching resource. When looking for new materials, she relies heavily on the Internet, where she has located numerous texts for classroom use. In addition, she has joined online message boards and an e-mail group from her graduate school, and she has recently begun investigating online courses or certification programs in order to continue her education.

| 8:3 Advocating |

Over time, Ezme feels less stress about teaching and has begun to enjoy recognition for her success in the classroom. Some teachers have commented recently that students seem to enjoy her class and make special note of the variety of activities that she uses. Because she is one of the few English teachers with a master's degree at her university, she has been asked to conduct workshops on differentiated assessment. One workshop in particular was a great success, so she submitted a paper about it to the Mexican Association of Teachers of English (MexTESOL). As her professional confidence increases, she also considers the possibility of conducting a collaborative research project with Hector to investigate the development of learning communities between paired classes.

Discussion

A. Study the vignette. List the formal and informal ways in which Ezme is developing professionally.

[Answer Key A: She finds a colleague to work with. She joins an online message board and an e-mail group from her graduate school. She conducts workshops. She presents at MexTESOL. She considers doing a research project.]

B. Discuss the following:

1. How would you go about finding a fellow teacher who would be open to and enthusiastic about cultivating a professional relationship like the one between Ezme and Hector?

2. It is clear that this teaching situation has been challenging for Ezme and she has worked hard at motivating herself to succeed. If she had not met Hector, how else might she have overcome her difficulties?

C. Ezme finds an issue that motivates her to research it further. What issue might motivate you to pursue research? What would you do in your class, or what discussions would you have, before undertaking such a project?

Appendixes

Appendix A
Supporting Documents

Best Practices: English as a Foreign Language Instruction to Adult Learners

Carla Chamberlin, Penn State Abington

"Best practice" is situated within a conceptualization of teaching and learning as socially constructed, multidimensional activities. The discourse of teacher education and adult second language teaching in the past decade reveals this perspective on the nature of teaching and learning in discussions of

- pedagogy and content knowledge

- knowledge of learners and contexts

- professional development, change, and reflection

- professional identity

- teaching as an interpretive activity

1) The nature of teaching

Current literature in second language teaching and learning challenges the traditional model of teaching in which teachers serve as neutral transmitters of information. A reconceptualized vision of teaching views the teacher as a participant in the process of teaching and learning. Teacher education, consequently, should not focus on behavioristic approaches but should view teaching as thinking and reasoning (Freeman & Richards, 1993).

Teaching involves multiple dimensions including how and what is taught in the classroom, how teachers understand learners and contexts, and how teachers understand their own roles in the teaching-learning process.

The underlying assumption in current thought is that there will be a positive relationship between student learning and teacher education that focuses on the development of the teacher as a participant and interpreter. Direct empirical evidence to support this link is lacking.

Challenging teachers to articulate and explore their values, beliefs, and motivation, teacher education has recently turned its attention to the questions of decision-making, reflection, and classroom inquiry as foci for teacher development and effective practice.

A framework that reconceptualizes the knowledge base of teacher education includes the cognitive and communicative processes that engage a person in teaching and connect the domains of "teacher as learner," "schools and schooling," and "the activity of teaching and learning" (Freeman & Johnson, 1998). This framework, which assumes firmly established disciplinary knowledge, proposes a broadened scope of teacher education.

2) Pedagogy and content knowledge

Although components of language are often examined separately, disciplinary knowledge is not necessarily viewed as the mastery of isolated bits of information. Teachers are expected to make connections and incorporate the acquisition of reading, writing, speaking, listening, and socio-cultural skills in a communicative and process-oriented approach to language learning. The *New Ways Series* published by Teachers of English to Speakers of Other Languages (TESOL) contains volumes that separately address areas including reading, grammar, computers, listening, and speaking, but point to the interconnectivity of disciplinary knowledge through student-centered, process-oriented activities.

Communication involves simultaneous and reciprocal interaction of verbal and nonverbal behaviors. An integrated view of communication is echoed in the literature about communicative competencies, but is not yet strongly integrated into approaches to teacher education.

Teachers' voices are central to pedagogy. *TeacherSource: A Professional Resource and Education Series* (Freeman, 1998) approaches professional issues by including narratives as "teacher's voice," theoretical foundations in "frameworks," and reader participation in "investigations." This consistency in format underlines the assumptions that teachers' voices are key to interpreting situations and that theory and application can be part of interpretation. The volumes themselves situate disciplinary and pedagogical knowledge within a framework that recognizes the beliefs and values of teachers and students.

Teachers must take greater responsibility in challenging the appropriateness and effectiveness of pedagogical methods and materials. Lin's (1999) work reminds us that teachers must understand the cultural capital of students in order to choose the best strategies for the audience, and Tarvin and Al-Arishi (1991) argue that many task- and process-oriented activities do not really allow for reflection. From an epistemological stance, Bell (1993) challenges the idea that "education," "literacy," and "progress" are neutral and asks if teachers even agree what the concepts mean for adult English as a second language (ESL) learners.

Culture is an essential component of language learning. Culture is not represented solely through objects, costumes, food, and historical tidbits, but also through the dynamics of intercultural communication (Fantini, 1997) and the relationship among individuals and social groups (Atkinson, 1999).

The content of language learning has expanded. Today's language teachers prepare students for professional, interpersonal, and computer-mediated interactions. Moreover, topics such as racism, class differences, dialects, and sexual orientation enter in the conversation (Nelson, 1993, 1999; Summerhawk, 1998).

3) Relationship to the audience (learners and place)

Teachers should have knowledge and understanding of learners and the contexts of teaching. This encompasses individual needs and learning styles, group dynamics, multicultural issues, learners' motivation, politics of the school, support of the community, and the status of English and learners in the school and community. Adult learners constitute a heterogeneous population for which many teachers are not prepared (Bell, 1993; Gillespie, 1993; Norton, 1997).

ESL teachers should be prepared to deal with the needs of adult learners who are coping with complex social and family networks, cultural adjustment in communities, and first language literacy (Bell, 1993; Gillespie, 1993; McKay & Wong, Eds., 2000; Tarone & Kuehn, 2000; Weinstein-Shr, 1993).

Teachers have control in establishing and maintaining patterns of communication in the classroom. Teachers should consider students' perceptions of classroom communication, classroom exchanges (teacher-student and student-student), and community- and materials-based issues (Johnson, 1995).

Teachers should recognize the strengths of second language speakers rather than viewing them as failed or incompetent language users, or holding them to the standards of native speakers. Language teaching, therefore, needs to emphasize the learner as an active user of the language and set goals appropriate to the needs of the students (Cook, 1999).

Teacher-student interactions are more effective for learning when negotiation for meaning takes place (Goldstein & Conrad, 1990).

The context of learning and teaching is a socially constructed environment with teachers and students both creating identities for themselves (Ibrahim, 1999; Norton, 1997; Smoke, 1998). Social interactions among students, teachers, administrators, parents, and community are part of the complex landscape of teaching (Johnson, 1999).

Teaching students in a university setting requires an understanding of the academic discourse community and the expectations that a nonnative speaker faces (Hamp-Lyons, 1997; Zamel & Spack, 1998). ESL teachers may need to participate in collaborative education with teachers of other subject areas to provide better academic opportunity for English for academic purposes (EAP) students (Kaufman & Brooks, 1996).

English for specific purposes, such as business, is in growing demand in a global economy (St. John & Johnson, 1996). Teachers should understand the needs of adult learners with specialized needs in unique contexts.

Adult learners of ESL can successfully engage in "transformational" learning—a process in which they examine their beliefs and values as they acquire new knowledge and experience change in their frames of reference (King, 2000; Mezirow, 1990, 1996).

4) Development, change, and reflection

Teacher "training" has shifted to teacher "development." Teaching is a cognitively complex activity that is not necessarily taught directly through skills training. Reflection and classroom-based research are tools for teachers to learn more about what they do in order to develop professionally (Richards & Nunan, 1990).

Teacher development is a process of exploring personal beliefs, principles, and theories and their relationship to knowledge, skills, and classroom practice (Gebhard & Oprandy, 1999).

Teachers can be responsible for their own teaching and collaborate with others to explore the nature of their work (Edge, 1992; Gebhard & Oprandy, 1999). Teachers, in fact, should be empowered to carry out their own classroom research and inquiry (Freeman, 1998).

Teachers can develop and move through a process of change by personalizing information, moving it through a change cycle, and incorporating it into teaching practice, eventually making it part of their belief system. Pennington's (1995) model applies a systemic approach to teacher development, recognizing how the personal and professional are integrated in an individual's perception of the world and played out in decision-making and practice.

Novice teachers face concerns and frustrations that may differ from more experienced teachers (Numrich, 1996).

Teachers' narrative reconstructions of their experiences as teachers and learners inform their practice and create awareness of the consequences of their actions. Teacher education should recognize personal practical knowledge as a means of building connections between coursework and experiential knowledge, encouraging reflection, and recognizing the role of emotions, beliefs, and stories in teacher development (Golombek, 1998).

Reflection is a key process in teaching practice. Reflective teachers can make sense of their work by understanding and articulating the interconnectedness of their personal experiences, their beliefs and values, and their decision-making processes in the classroom (Bell, 1993; Freeman, 1991; Stanley, 1998).

5) Professional identity

Preparation for professional situations should be a part of teacher education because ESL teachers who find themselves in a variety of contexts must develop different professional identities (Johnston, 1997; Liu, 1999).

Preparation for adult ESL literacy teachers must validate the wide range of experiences that teachers bring to the classroom as it establishes professionalism (Crandall, 1993).

Nonnative speaking teachers of English sometimes find themselves disempowered because of the identity and power relationships between themselves and native-speaker teachers (Amin, 1997; Liu, 1999; Norton, 1997; Tang, 1997).

6) Teachers as interpreters

Teachers make sense of their world and the social contexts of their work. Creating opportunities for collaboration, reflection, and theorizing is optimal for teacher education (Johnson, 2000).

Learning to teach is a process, and the teacher-learner brings something to this process. Teacher education should emphasize how teachers make sense of what they do rather than offering prescriptions of what to do (Freeman & Cornwell, 1993).

Teachers are capable of doing their own research. The union of teaching and research helps teachers articulate their understanding of what they do, as well as offering them more credibility as experts (Freeman, 1998).

Teaching is a situated and interpretive activity that requires reasoning to examine the interconnectedness of the various aspects of context. Reasoning involves more than just thinking about an event; it also involves how teachers think about an event within the context of their own classrooms (Johnson, 1999).

References

Amin, N. (1997). Race and the identity of the nonnative ESL teacher. *TESOL Quarterly, 31,* 580–583.

Atkinson, D. (1999). TESOL and culture. *TESOL Quarterly, 33,* 625–654.

Bell, J. S. (1993). Discussions of Kerfoot and Wrigley: The teacher as bridge between program and practice. *TESOL Quarterly, 27,* 467–475.

Cook, V. (1999). Going beyond the native speaker in language teaching. *TESOL Quarterly, 33,* 185–209.

Crandall, J. (1993). Professionalism of adult ESL literacy. *TESOL Quarterly, 27,* 497–515.

Edge, J. (1992). *Cooperative development: Professional self-development through cooperation with colleagues.* New York: Longman.

Fantini, A. (Ed.) (1997). *New ways in teaching culture.* Alexandria, VA: TESOL, Inc.

Freeman, D. (1991). "To make the tacit explicit": Teacher education, emerging discourse, and conceptions of teaching. *Teaching and Teacher Education, 7*(5/6), 439–454.

Freeman, D. (1998). *Doing teacher research: From inquiry to understanding.* New York: Heinle & Heinle

Freeman, D. (Series Ed.) (1998). *TeacherSource: A professional resource and teacher education series.* New York: Heinle & Heinle.

Freeman, D., & Cornwell, S. (1993). *New ways in teacher education.* Alexandria, VA: TESOL, Inc.

Freeman, D., & Johnson, K. E. (1998). Reconceptualizing the knowledge-base of language teacher education. *TESOL Quarterly, 32,* 397–417.

Freeman, D., & Richards, J. C. (1993). Conceptions of teaching and the education of second language teachers. *TESOL Quarterly, 27,* 193–216.

Gebhard, J. G., & Oprandy, R. (1999). *Language teaching awareness: A guide to exploring beliefs and practices.* New York: Cambridge.

Gillespie, M. (1993). Profiles of adult learners: Revealing the multiple faces of literacy. *TESOL Quarterly, 27,* 529–533.

Goldstein, L. M., & Conrad, S. M. (1990). Student input and negotiation of meaning in ESL writing conferences. *TESOL Quarterly, 24*(3), 443–460.

Golombek, P. R. (1998). A study of language teachers' personal practical knowledge. *TESOL Quarterly, 32,* 447–464.

Hamp-Lyons, L. (Ed.). (1997). English for academic purposes [Special issue]. *English for Specific Purposes, 16*(1).

Ibrahim, A. (1999). Becoming black: Rap and hip-hop, race, gender, identity, and the politics of ESL learning. *TESOL Quarterly, 33,* 349–369.

Johnson, K. E. (1995). *Understanding communication in second language classrooms.* New York: Cambridge.

Johnson, K. E. (1999). *Understanding language teaching: Reasoning in action.* New York: Heinle & Heinle.

Johnson, K. E. (Ed.). (2000). *Teacher education.* Washington, DC: TESOL, Inc.

Johnston, B. (1997). Do EFL teachers have careers? *TESOL Quarterly, 31*(4), 681–712.

Kaufman, D., & Brooks, J. G. (1996). Interdisciplinary collaboration in teacher education. *TESOL Quarterly, 30*(2), 231–251.

King, K. P. (2000). The adult ESL experience: Facilitating perspective transformation in the classroom. *Adult Basic Education, 10*(2), 69–89.

Lin, A. M. Y. (1999). Doing-English-lessons in the reproduction or transformation of social worlds? *TESOL Quarterly, 33,* 393–412.

Liu, J. (1999). Nonnative-English-speaking professionals in TESOL. *TESOL Quarterly, 33*(1), 85–102.

McKay, S. L., & Wong, S. C. (Eds.). (2000). *New immigrants in the United States.* New York: Cambridge.

Mezirow, J. (1990). *Fostering critical reflection in adulthood: A guide to transformative and emancipatory learning.* San Francisco: Jossey-Bass.

Mezirow, J. (1996). Toward a learning theory of adult literacy. *Adult Basic Education, 6*(3), 115–126.

Murphy, J. M. (1991). Oral communication in TESOL: Integrating speaking, listening, and pronunciation. *TESOL Quarterly, 25*(1), 51–75.

Nelson, C. (1993). Heterosexism in ESL: Examining our attitudes. *TESOL Quarterly, 27,* 143–150.

Nelson, C. (1999). Sexual identities in ESL: Queer theory and classroom inquiry. *TESOL Quarterly, 33,* 371–391.

Norton, B. (1997). Language, identity, and the ownership of English. *TESOL Quarterly, 31*(3), 409–429.

Numrich, C. (1996). On becoming a language teacher: Insights from diary studies. *TESOL Quarterly, 30,* 131–151.

Pennington, M. C. (1995). The teacher change cycle. *TESOL Quarterly, 29,* 705–731.

Richards, J. C. (Series Ed.) (19–). *New Ways in TESOL Series II.* Alexandria, VA: TESOL, Inc.

Richards, J., & Nunan, D. (Eds.). (1990). *Second language teacher education.* New York: Cambridge.

St. John, M. J., & Johnson, C. (Eds.). (1996). Business English [Special Issue]. *English for Specific Purposes, 15*(1).

Smoke, T. (Ed.) (1998). *Adult ESL: Politics, pedagogy, and participation in classroom and community programs.* Mahwah, NJ: Lawrence Erlbaum.

Stanley, C. (1998). A framework for teacher reflectivity. *TESOL Quarterly, 32,* 584–591.

Summerhawk, B. (1998). From closet to classroom: Gay issues in ESL/EFL. *The Language Teacher, 22*(5), 21–23.

Tang, C. (1997). On the power and status of nonnative ESL teachers. *TESOL Quarterly, 31*(3), 577–583.

Tarvin, W. L., & Al-Arishi, A. Y. (1991). Rethinking communicative language teaching: Reflection and the EFL classroom. *TESOL Quarterly, 25,* 9–27.

Weinstein-Shr, G. (1993). Overview discussion: Directions in adult ESL literacy—an invitation to dialogue. *TESOL Quarterly, 27,* 517–528.

Zamel, V., & Spack, R. (Eds.). (1998). *Negotiating academic literacies: Teaching and learning across languages and cultures.* Mahwah, NJ: Lawrence Erlbaum.

Performance-Based Assessment in Teacher Education: A Summary

Bill Johnston, Indiana University

This summary is organized into three parts. Part I outlines the principal qualities and characteristics of performance-based assessment (PBA) in teacher education. Part II enumerates common practices in PBA and principles underlying them. Part III mentions some of the key issues surrounding the relationship between PBA and teacher education reform. To facilitate use, the summary is presented largely in the form of bulleted lists.

Part I: Characteristics of Performance-Based Assessment

Broadly speaking, PBA encompasses a student's ability to integrate and apply learning across disciplines through some performance task (Mihalevich & Carr, 1998, p. 72). PBA is linked with the use of standards in teacher education, which describe what teachers should know and be able to do rather than listing courses that teachers should take in order to be awarded a license (INTASC, 2001).

The following list is not merely a description of forms of PBA, but should also be read as a set of guidelines. That is, it describes what PBA *should* look like, thus simultaneously raising certain key issues and problems. This said, PBA can be characterized by the following qualities:

- It involves authentic forms of assessment relating to teaching, rather than decontextualized tasks such as multiple-choice formats.

- In it, assessment is linked to performance: that is, to what a teacher can *do*.

- It involves multiple assessments and the integration of complex evidence, rather than one-shot, simplistic testing.

- It involves multiple *kinds* of assessment, for example a combination of tests and portfolio assessment (Darling-Hammond et al., 1998). In addition, there is an emphasis on both tasks beyond the classroom (e.g., dealing with parents, taking part in professional meetings) and classroom-based tasks.

- It represents progress, acknowledging a teacher's growth over time (what Diez and Hass, 1997, p. 21, call assessment-as-learning) and the need to treat teachers at different career stages differently.

- It is sensitive to context and to the fact that different teachers may have different needs.

- It incorporates self-assessment.

- It incorporates a strong reflective component.

- It involves a strong component of collaboration.

- It is supportive of, and congruent with, forms of teacher research such as Action Research (Diez & Blackwell, 1999, p. 353).

Part II: Practices

The Web site of the National Board for Professional Teaching Standards (NBPTS) lists the following broad principles to be followed in developing assessment procedures:

- Tasks should be authentic and, therefore, complex.

- Tasks should be open ended, allowing teachers to show their own practice.

- Tasks should encourage analysis and reflection.

- Subject-matter knowledge should underlie all performances.

- Tasks should encourage teachers to exemplify good practice.

- Each task should assess a cluster of standards.

- Each standard should be assessed by more than one task. (NBPTS, 2001)

With the above-mentioned qualities and characteristics in mind, PBA typically involves the following kinds of practice:

- portfolios

- reflective components such as reflective journals

- videotapes of teaching

- authentic and simulated teaching tasks

- authentic and simulated authentic interaction with colleagues, students, and parents

- close collaborative work with mentor teachers as well as faculty (Nelms & Thomas, 1998)

- preparation of a teaching unit

- projects

- exhibitions

- on-demand performance tasks (Lowe & Banker, 1998, p. 54)

- structured observations

- self-evaluation

Furthermore, assessment is holistic; it is not carried out mechanically and automatically, but with regard for the particular candidate, his or her situation, and his or her past and future growth.

To sum up, the NBPTS recommends that any assessment meet five requirements that they label the APPLE criteria:

- Administratively feasible

- Professionally acceptable

- Publicly credible

- Legally defensible

- Economically affordable (NBPTS, 2001)

Part III: Performance-Based Assessment and Reform

Performance-based assessment of teachers has become much more widespread in teacher education following the reforms of the last 15 years. Three sets of standards for teachers embrace these assessments: National Council for Accreditation of Teacher Education (NCATE) for teacher education, Interstate New Teacher Assessment and Support Consortium (INTASC) for teacher licensure, and NBPTS for experienced teachers. PBA models have been adopted by many schools and in many states. These reforms are largely considered successful: Darling-Hammond et al. (1998) claim for example, that the reforms in Connecticut have eliminated teacher shortages while increasing teachers' knowledge and skills and improving education for children (p. 35). It seems clear that the kinds of practices involved are indeed likely to lead to enhanced teacher learning. Nevertheless, the literature mentions a number of caveats, which must be considered in the shift to PBA of teachers and teacher candidates. I enumerate here the most significant of these.

- Diez and Hass (1997) emphasize that the shift to PBA cannot properly be achieved within the traditional teacher education program of freestanding courses. Rather, this shift necessarily involves a transformation (p. 17) of the program itself. Without such a transformation—if PBA is regarded merely as an add-on (p. 17)—reform efforts will be seriously compromised if not largely ineffective. In the same vein, Nelms and Thomas (1998) speak of performance-based instruction (p. 85) as a complementary process of PBA. Lowe and Banker (1998) explain that a teacher education program using a PBA approach should include the following components: authentic assessment, cooperative learning, block scheduling of courses, extended field experiences, interdisciplinary instruction, integration of technology, and the development and use of portfolios (p. 56). These components are also instructive for envisioning how PBA can impact a program as a whole.

- PBA can only work when it is supported by a certain set of *assumptions* and *values* concerning the nature and purpose of assessment that are consonant with the position outlined in this summary (Henn-Reinke & Kies, 1998).

- Another critical issue is that of local ownership. Diez and Hass (1997) argue that in this case it *is* necessary to reinvent the wheel: that is, that each local setting should work through the issues and processes of PBA, rather than blindly adopting frameworks from elsewhere (p. 18).

- Mihalevich and Carr (1998) warn of the obstacles posed by the faculty "nay-sayer" who is resistant to change, and also by the "natural discomfort" of change (p. 75).

- PBA can only work if the standards of performance expected of candidates are clearly and explicitly laid out. By the same token, these standards must be made available to the candidates so they are fully aware of what is expected of them and of the criteria of success. (For examples of articulated expectations, see Nelms & Thomas, 1998, p. 83; Diez & Hass, 1997, p. 20; Durden & Hunt, 1998, pp. 90–91 and pp. 94–95; Heuwinkel & Hagerty, 1998, p. 114. Organizations such as NCATE and INTASC also offer articulations of standards on their respective Web sites.)

- Also of critical importance is the need to continue to rethink and reexamine measurement practices and techniques. PBA offers a radically new way of thinking about what it is to be a good teacher, but it still involves a form of psychometrics in which individuals are measured. Darling-Hammond et al. (1998) point out that subjectivity can make the measurements involved in PBA unreliable and invalid, and that much work remains to be done to ensure that assessments are fair, accurate, and useful.

- Much more than in other kinds of teacher assessment, schools play an important role, and any reform efforts hinge crucially on effective collaboration between universities and schools (Lowe & Banker, 1998, p. 57).

- Common problems shifting to PBA include lack of time, administrative restrictions, insufficient resources, and clashes between university and school cultures (Rude, 1998, pp. 104–107).

- Above all, according to Diez and Hass (1997), "what is needed is to break out of the knowledge box," that is, to supplement the question of "What does the teacher need to know?" with questions such as "What would the teacher *do* with that knowledge?" and "*Why* is that knowledge essential to the teacher's practice?" (p. 19).

References

Darling-Hammond, L., Diez, M. E., Moss, P., Pecheone, R., Pullin, D., Schafer, W. D., & Vickers, L. (1998). The role of standards and assessment: A dialogue. In M. E. Diez (Ed.), *Changing the practice of teacher education: Standards and assessment as a lever for change* (pp. 11–38). Washington, DC: American Association of Colleges for Teacher Education.

Diez, M. E. (Ed.) (1998). *Changing the practice of teacher education. Standards and assessment as a lever for change.* Washington, DC: American Association of Colleges for Teacher Education.

Diez, M. E., & Blackwell, P. (1999). Improving master's education for practicing teachers: The impact of the National Board for Professional Teaching Standards. *Teaching and Change, 6,* 350–363.

Diez, M. E., & Hass, J. M. (1997). No more piecemeal reform: Using performance-based approaches to rethink teacher education. *Action in Teacher Education, 19*(2), 17–26.

Diez, M. E., & Hass, J. M., Henn-Reinke, K., Stoffels, J. A., & Truchan, L. C. (1998). Guiding coherence: Performance-based teacher education at Alverno College. In M. E. Diez (Ed.), *Changing the practice of teacher education: Standards and assessment as a lever for change* (pp. 41–40). Washington, DC: American Association of Colleges for Teacher Education.

Durden, D., & Hunt, A. (1998). Outcomes and assessment in language arts and mathematics. In M. E. Diez (Ed.), *Changing the practice of teacher education: Standards assessment as a lever for change* (pp. 89–97). Washington, DC: American Association of Colleges for Teacher Education.

Henn-Reinke, K., & Kies, K. M. (1998). Institutionalizing a standards-based approach to teaching, learning, and assessment. In M. E. Diez (Ed.), *Changing the practice of teacher education: Standards and assessment as a lever for change* (pp. 157–167). Washington, DC: American Association of Colleges for Teacher Education.

Heuwinkel, M., & Hagerty, P. J. (1998). The development of a standards-based assessment plan in a school-university partnership. In M. E. Diez (Ed.), *Changing the practice of teacher education: Standards and assessment as a lever for change* (pp. 111–120). Washington, DC: American Association of Colleges for Teacher Education.

INTASC (Interstate New Teacher Assessment and Support Consortium). (2001). Web site: <http://www .ccsso.org/Projects/interstate_new_teacher_assessment_and_support_consortium/780.cfm>, accessed 4/14/08.

Lowe, V. J., & Banker, B. J. (1998). Preparing teachers at Asbury College: Restructuring for the 21st century. In M. E. Diez (Ed.), *Changing the practice of teacher education: Standards and assessment as a lever for change* (pp. 51–60). Washington, DC: American Association of Colleges for Teacher Education.

Mihalevich, C. D., & Carr, K. S. (1998). One university's journey toward teacher education restructuring. In M. E. Diez (Ed.), *Changing the practice of teacher education: Standards and assessment as a lever for change* (pp. 71–79). Washington, DC: American Association of Colleges for Teacher Education.

NBPTS (National Board for Professional Teaching Standards). (2001): Web site: http://www.nbpts .org/, accessed 8/11/01.

NCATE (National Council for Accreditation of Teacher Education). (2001). Web site: http://www.ncate .org/, accessed 8/11/01.

Nelms, V. C., & Thomas, M. G. (1998). Assessment: A process. In M. E. Diez (Ed.), *Changing the practice of teacher education: Standards and assessment as a lever for change* (pp. 81–88). Washington, DC: American Association of Colleges for Teacher Education.

Rude, H. (1998). Structures which support changing processes and outcomes in teacher education. In M. E. Diez (Ed.), *Changing the practice of teacher education. Standards and assessment as a lever for change* (pp. 99–109). Washington, DC: American Association of Colleges for Teacher Education.

Appendix B
Performance Criteria

Standard 1: Planning

Teachers plan instruction to promote learning and meet learner goals, and modify plans to assure learner engagement and achievement.

	Observation Measures or Self-Review	Possible Interview or Discussion
	The instructor or candidate	
1:1 Overall Planning	☑ approaches criteria ☐ meets criteria ☐ exceeds criteria	
	☐ identifies and articulates short- and long-term plans to promote learning ☐ identifies and articulates learning goals for both language and other content	*What considerations might you have in short- and long-term planning?*
1:2 Learner Considerations	☐ approaches criteria ☑ meets criteria ☐ exceeds criteria	
	☑ identifies learners' interests and integrates in planning ☑ identifies learners' needs and integrates in planning ☑ identifies learners' prior learning and background knowledge and integrates in planning	*While planning, what considerations might you have regarding the learner? Please give examples.*
1:3 Lesson Planning	☑ approaches criteria ☑ meets criteria ☐ exceeds criteria	
	☐ develops lesson plans that allow time for learning, review, and assessment ☑ develops lesson plans that include assessments to evaluate learning and achievement of objectives ☐ develops lesson plans that connect individual lessons to curriculum and to program objectives	*What elements should a lesson plan include?*
1:4 Activities and Strategies	☐ approaches criteria ☐ meets criteria ☐ exceeds criteria	
	☑ designs or sequences strategies and activities to deliver content ☑ designs or sequences strategies and activities to address individual differences ☑ designs or sequences strategies and activities to accomplish learning objectives ☑ designs or sequences strategies and activities that build on learners' problem-solving and critical-thinking skills ☑ designs or sequences strategies and activities that employ more than one variety of English ☑ designs or sequences strategies and activities that encourage learners to use English beyond the classroom	*How do you choose the activities and strategies for a given lesson plan?*
1:5 Resources	☐ approaches criteria ☐ meets criteria ☐ exceeds criteria	
	☑ selects appropriate resources	*Please give examples of resources that can enhance instruction.*

Standard 2: Instructing

Teachers create supportive environments that engage all learners in purposeful learning and promote respectful classroom interactions.

	Observation Measures and Self-Review	Possible Interview or Discussion
	The instructor or candidate	
2:1 Classroom Management	❑ approaches criteria ❑ meets criteria ☑ exceeds criteria	
	☑ organizes and manages constructive interactions ☑ creates an environment that engages all learners ☑ makes effective use of classroom time ☑ manages activities ☑ adjusts instruction when necessary ☑ uses unexpected events to extend learning	*What classroom management techniques do you use?* *What do you do when a lesson is not working as planned?*
2:2 Instructor Role	❑ approaches criteria ☑ meets criteria ❑ exceeds criteria	
	☑ makes goals explicit ☑ gives clear instructions ☑ promotes learner participation ☑ listens and responds to learner talk ☑ models natural language use ☑ models and promotes respectful interactions among learners ☑ asks questions to check for comprehension ☑ facilitates discussion ☑ clarifies student thinking ☑ gives corrective feedback	*How are you a good model for your students?* *What can you do to ensure learner participation and interaction?*
2:3 Activities and Strategies	❑ approaches criteria ☑ meets criteria ❑ exceeds criteria	
	☑ uses a variety of strategies and activities to introduce, explain, and restate concepts and processes ☑ uses a variety of strategies and activities to address individual differences ☑ uses a variety of strategies and activities to group learners in a variety of ways to meet goals ☑ uses a variety of strategies and activities to make content accessible ☑ uses a variety of strategies and activities to further critical-thinking skills	*What strategies do you use to make activities accessible to all students?* *How do you address a variety of learning styles and individual differences when choosing and managing activities?*
2:4 Learner Considerations	❑ approaches criteria ❑ meets criteria ☑ exceeds criteria	
	☑ treats learners as adults ☑ conveys and maintains expectations for learner behavior ☑ engages learners in decision-making about their learning ☑ helps learners become independent, lifelong learners	*What learning goals other than specific performance objectives do you have for your students?*

Standard 3: Assessing

Teachers recognize the importance of and are able to gather and interpret information about learning and performance to promote the continuous intellectual and linguistic development of each learner. Teachers use knowledge of student performance to make decisions about planning and instruction "on the spot" and for the future. Teachers involve learners in determining what will be assessed and provide constructive feedback to learners, based on assessments of their learning.

	Observation Measures and Self-Review	Possible Interview or Discussion
	The instructor or candidate	
3:1 Need for Assessment	❑ approaches criteria ❑ meets criteria ☑ exceeds criteria	
	☑ demonstrates a recognition of the importance of obtaining information about learner performance ☑ ties assessment to learning objectives	*Why is assessment important?*
3:2 Types of Assessment	❑ approaches criteria ☑ meets criteria ❑ exceeds criteria	
	☑ uses a variety of formal and informal assessment tools appropriate for the context and desired results ☑ uses assessment that is multimodal, systematic, and purposeful ☑ uses assessment tools that allow learners to demonstrate their learning ☑ uses assessment tools that are culturally sensitive, appropriate, and equitable ☑ uses assessment tools that are instructor generated and standardized	*What different types of assessment tools might you incorporate?* *What might you consider in developing the tools to assess every student appropriately?*
3:3 Evaluation of Results	❑ approaches criteria ☑ meets criteria ❑ exceeds criteria	
	☑ gathers and interprets information about learner background, preferences, expectations, and goals ☑ monitors learning as it happens in the classroom ☑ gathers, interprets, and documents information about performance before, during, and after instruction	*When do you evaluate assessment results and how do you incorporate those results into instruction?*
3:4 Learner Considerations	❑ approaches criteria ☑ meets criteria ❑ exceeds criteria	
	☑ engages learners in self-assessment and monitoring of their progress ☑ uses learner feedback on instructional methods and approaches in the design of appropriate assessments ☑ provides constructive feedback to learners based on assessments of their learning	*How do you engage learners in assessment?*
3:5 Development and Changes	❑ approaches criteria ☑ meets criteria ❑ exceeds criteria	
	❑ evaluates the reliability and validity of instructor-generated and standardized assessment instruments ☑ uses assessment results and learner feedback to adjust or modify the future learning objectives	*How can assessment affect instruction?*

Standard 4: Identity and Context

Teachers understand the importance of who learners are and how their communities, backgrounds, and goals shape learning and expectations of learning. Teachers recognize how context contributes to identity formation and therefore influences learning. Teachers use this knowledge of identity and settings in planning, instructing, and assessing.

	Observation Measures and Self-Review	Possible Interview or Discussion
	The instructor or candidate	
4:1 Classroom Environment	❑ approaches criteria ❑ meets criteria ☑ exceeds criteria	
	☑ creates an environment conducive to adult learning ☑ acknowledges learners as adults ❑ establishes classroom routines and encourages learners' appreciation for each other	*Describe your classroom environment and give examples of how it is conducive to adult learning.*
4:2 Learner Identities	❑ approaches criteria ❑ meets criteria ☑ exceeds criteria	
	☑ respects the legitimacy and diversity of identities and roles' impact on planning, instructing, and assessing ☑ uses the diversity of adult learners' identities and roles as a classroom resource ☑ varies instructional practices to address learner identities and roles	*How might the diversity of your students impact planning, instructing, and assessing?*
4:3 Instructor Interaction	❑ approaches criteria ❑ meets criteria ☑ exceeds criteria	
	☑ interacts equitably and responsibly with adult learners ☑ models respectful attitudes toward cross-cultural differences and conflicts	*How can instructor and student interaction promote respect for cultural differences?*
4:4 Learner Communities	❑ approaches criteria ❑ meets criteria ☑ exceeds criteria	
	☑ helps learners connect and apply their learning to home, community, and workplace ☑ integrates information from learners' communities in planning, instructing, and assessing ☑ seeks out and uses knowledge about learner communities to guide instructional practice	*How can you use knowledge about the learners' communities to guide instructional practices?*

Standard 5: Language Proficiency

Teachers demonstrate proficiency in social, business/workplace, and academic English. Proficiency in speaking, listening, reading, and writing means that a teacher is functionally equivalent to a native speaker with some higher education.

	Observation Measures and Self-Review	Possible Interview or Discussion
5:1 General Proficiency	*The instructor or candidate*	
	❑ approaches criteria ❑ meets criteria ☑ exceeds criteria	
5:2 Other Contexts	☑ demonstrates proficiency in oral, written, and professional English ☑ demonstrates proficiency in social, academic, and professional English	*What is your experience speaking and writing English in a variety of contexts including social, academic, and professional?*
	❑ approaches criteria ❑ meets criteria ☑ exceeds criteria	
5:3 Classroom Performance	❑ demonstrates familiarity with more than one variety of English ❑ varies register according to context	*Do you think it is important to help students communicate in a variety of registers? Why or why not?*
	❑ approaches criteria ❑ meets criteria ☑ exceeds criteria	
5:4 Nonnative Advocate	☑ serves as an English language model for learners	*What do you consider effective English language models for learners in your classroom?*
	❑ approaches criteria ❑ meets criteria ☑ exceeds criteria	
	☑ explains and advocates for NNES teachers	*Do you think that nonnative speakers can be effective ESL/EFL instructors? Why or why not?*

Standard 6: Learning

Teachers draw on their knowledge of language and adult language learning to understand the processes by which learners acquire a new language in and out of classroom settings. They use this knowledge to support adult language learning.

	Observation Measures and Self-Review	Possible Interview or Discussion
6:1 Classroom Environment	*The instructor or candidate*	
	☐ approaches criteria ☑ meets criteria ☐ exceeds criteria	
	☑ creates classroom contexts in which language acquisition can take place ☑ scaffolds language and content ☑ integrates instruction in oral language and literacy ☑ adjusts teacher talk to the English level of the learner ☑ provides language input, feedback, and opportunities for learners to use and extend English	*Please describe your classroom environment. What do you do, and how do your students respond?*
6:2 Learner Activity	☐ approaches criteria ☑ meets criteria ☐ exceeds criteria	
	☑ provides learning experiences that promote autonomy and choice ☑ provides learning experiences that promote cooperation and collaboration ☑ creates classroom contexts in which learners can negotiate meaning through interactions with the teacher and with one another ☑ creates situations where meaningful messages are exchanged ☑ encourages learners to use their first language skills and abilities as a resource for learning English ☑ helps learners to develop metacognitive awareness and use strategies for knowing about, reflecting on, and monitoring their own language	*How would you describe a learner-centered classroom?* *What are the benefits of having a learner-centered classroom?*
6:3 Learner Variables	☐ approaches criteria ☑ meets criteria ☐ exceeds criteria	
	☑ demonstrates understanding of the personal and contextual factors that affect language learning ☑ provides learning experiences that respond to differential rates and styles of learning	*What variables affect language learning?*

Standard 7: Content

Teachers understand that language learning is most likely to occur when learners are trying to use the language for genuine communicative purposes. Teachers understand that the content of the language course is the language that learners need in order to discuss, listen to, read, and write about a subject or content area. Teachers design their lessons to help learners acquire the language they need to successfully communicate in the subject or content areas about which they want or need to learn.

	Observation Measures and Self-Review	Possible Interview or Discussion
7:1 Input and Practice	*The instructor or candidate*	
	❑ approaches criteria ❑ meets criteria ❑ exceeds criteria	
	❑ provides a model of oral and written language in the content area ❑ provides input and practice in the different linguistic features of the language used in the content area ❑ provides input and practice in the discourse structures used in the content area ❑ provides input and practice in applying sociocultural rules that relate to the content area ❑ provides input and practice in coping strategies that can be used when grammatical, sociocultural, and discourse competency is not fully developed	*What coping strategies can you teach students when they do not have sufficiently developed skills to carry on a conversation?*
7:2 Tasks in Content Area	❑ approaches criteria ❑ meets criteria ❑ exceeds criteria	
	❑ incorporates real-world tasks that give learners instruction and practice in doing activities specific to the content area in the four skill areas ❑ incorporates pedagogical tasks that give learners instruction and practice in using the language they need to successfully complete a real-world task	*Can you give examples of real-world tasks or projects that you have used in your classroom?*
7:3 Content Knowledge and Lesson Planning	❑ approaches criteria ❑ meets criteria ❑ exceeds criteria	
	❑ uses prior knowledge or expertise in content area to develop lessons ❑ collaborates with content specialists to develop lessons ❑ teaches students investigative or research strategies to acquire content knowledge on their own	*What can you do if you don't have the necessary content knowledge for a specific lesson?*

Standard 8: Commitment and Professionalism

Teachers continue to develop their understanding of the relationships between second language teaching and learning through the community of English language teaching professionals, the broader teaching community, and the community at large. This knowledge, in turn, informs and changes both the teachers and the communities.

	Observation Measures and Self-Review	Possible Interview or Discussion
	The instructor or candidate	
8:1 Gaining and Using Knowledge	☐ approaches criteria ☐ meets criteria ☑ exceeds criteria	
	☑ seeks out, interacts, and reflects on learning in teaching and learning communities and shares information with the teaching profession ☑ seeks out, interacts, and reflects on student learning and shares with teaching and learning communities ☑ seeks out, interacts, and reflects on knowledge about learners' communities and shares with teaching and learning communities ☑ pursues other opportunities to grow professionally	*Please give examples of teaching strategies or other things you have learned about the profession and how you have shared this information with others.*
8:2 Skill Development	☐ approaches criteria ☐ meets criteria ☑ exceeds criteria	
	☑ is developing his or her professional voice ☑ is developing personal professional development plans ☑ continually develops his or her knowledge and skills to improve instructional practices ☑ balances professional responsibilities with personal needs	*Are you actively involved in Teachers of English to Speakers of Other Languages (TESOL), any of its affiliates, or other organizations?* *What do you do to develop your teaching skills?*
8:3 Advocating	☐ approaches criteria ☑ meets criteria ☐ exceeds criteria	
	☑ advocates for English language teachers and English adult learners in his or her teaching context ☑ builds relationships with the teaching and learning communities to support students' learning and well-being ☐ encourages social and political strength in learners and their communities ☐ serves as a professional resource in all learning and teaching communities	*Are you involved professionally in your community?*

Appendix C
Resources and Additional Reading

Adelson-Goldstein, J., & Owensby, J. (2005). *An objective approach to lesson planning.* Los Angeles, CA: ESL/CBET & Citizenship Programs, Division of Adult and Career Education, Los Angeles Unified School District.

Ananda, S. (2000). *Equipped for the future assessment report: How instructors can support adult learners through performance-based assessment* (EX 0110P). Washington, DC: National Institute for Literacy.

Auerback, E. (1994). *Making meaning, making change: Participatory curriculum development for adult ESL literacy.* Washington, DC: Center for Applied Linguistics and Delta Systems. (ERIC Document Reproduction Service No. ED356688).

Belzer, A. (2005). Improving professional development systems: Recommendations from the Pennsylvania Adult Basic and Literacy Education Professional Development System Evaluation. *Adult Basic Education, 15*(1), 33–35.

Belzer, A., Drennon, C., & Smith, C. (2001). Building professional development systems in adult basic education: Lessons from the field. *Review of Adult Learning and Literacy, 2.* Available at www.ncsall .net/?id=559

Burns, A., & de Silva Joyce, H. (Eds.). (2007). *Planning and teaching creatively within a required curriculum for adults.* Alexandria, VA: TESOL.

Butler, S. M. (2003). Designing a technology-based science lesson: Student teachers grapple with an authentic problem of practice. *Journal of Technology and Teacher Education, 11*(4), 463–481.

California Department of Education. (1992). *English-as-a-second-language model standards for adult education programs.* Sacramento, CA: Author.

Carroll, M. (Ed.). (2007). *Developing a new curriculum for adult learners.* Alexandria, VA: TESOL.

Claussen, D. (2005). *Northwest Practitioner Knowledge Institute: Practitioner knowledge documentation.* Cambridge, MA: National Center for the Study of Adult Learning and Literacy. Available from www.ncsall.net

Coombe, C. A., & Hubley, N. J. (Eds.). (2003). *Assessment practices.* Alexandria, VA: TESOL.

Condelli, L., Wrigley, H. S., Yoon, K., Cronen, S., & Seburn, M. (2003). *What works: Study for adult ESL literacy students.* Unpublished manuscript.

Crandall, J. A. (1993). Professionalism and professionalization of adult ESL literacy. *TESOL Quarterly, 27,* 497–515.

Crandall, J. A. (1994). *Creating a professional workforce in adult ESL literacy.* Washington, DC: Center for Applied Linguistics. Available at http://www.cal.org/caela/esl_resources/digests/CRANDALL.html

Crandall, J. A., Ingersoll, G., and Lopez, J. (2008). *Adult ESL teacher credentialing and certification*. Washington, DC: Center for Applied Linguistics. Retrieved March 30, 2008, from http://www.cal.org /caela/esl_resources/briefs/tchrcred.html

Crandall, J. A., & Peyton, J. K. (Eds.). (1993). *Approaches to adult ESL literacy instruction*. Washington, DC & McHenry, IL: Center for Applied Linguistics and Delta Systems. Available from http://eric.ed.gov /ERICWebPortal/contentdelivery/servlet/ERICServlet?accno=ED364127

Florez, M. (2001). *Reflective teaching practice in adult ESL settings*. Washington, DC: Center for Applied Linguistics. Available at http://www.cal.org/caela/esl_resources/digests/reflect.html

Florez, M. A. (2002). *Content standards in adult ESL*. Washington, DC: Center for Applied Linguistics. Available at http://www.cal.org/caela/esl_resources/bibliographies/constanbib.html

Freeman, D., & Johnson, K. (1998). Reconceptualizing the knowledge base of language teacher education. *TESOL Quarterly, 32*, 397–417.

Friedenberg, J., Kennedy, D., Lomperis, A., Martin, W., & Westerfield, K. (2003). *Effective practices in workplace language training*. Alexandria, VA: TESOL.

Gerdes, C., & Wilberschied, L. (2003). Workplace ESL: Effective adaptations to fill a growing need. *TESOL Journal, 12*, 41–46.

Guskey, T. (2002). Does it make a difference? Evaluating professional development. *Educational Leadership*. 59(6), 45-51.

Hawk, W. B. (2000). *Online professional development for adult ESL educators*. Washington, DC: Center for Applied Linguistics. Available at http://www.cal.org/caela/esl_resources/briefs/onlinepd.html

Henrichsen, L. E. (Ed.). (2001). *Distance-learning programs*. Alexandria, VA: TESOL.

Lewis, M. (Ed.). (1997). *New ways in teaching adults*. Alexandria, VA: TESOL.

Maryland State Board of Education. (n.d.). *Maryland Adult ESL Program Standards*. Baltimore, MD: Author. Retrieved June 23, 2008, from http://www.umbc.edu/alrc/Standards/Texts/MdESLStand.html

Massachusetts Department of Education. (n.d.). *Adult (basic) education credential information by state*. Boston, MA: Author. Retrieved January 7, 2008, from www.doe.mass.edu/acls/abecert/abecred.xls

National Center for Family Literacy & Center for Applied Linguistics. (2004). *Practitioner toolkit: Working with adult English language learners*. Louisville, KY and Washington, DC: Authors. Available at http:// www.cal.org/caela/tools/instructional/prac_toolkit.html

Nunan, D., & Lamb, C. (1996). *The self-directed teacher*. New York: Cambridge University Press.

Orr, T. (2002). *English for specific purposes*. Alexandria, VA: TESOL.

Peyton, J. K. (2005). *Using the ESL program standards to evaluate and improve adult ESL programs*. Washington, DC: Center for Applied Linguistics. Retrieved January 7, 2008, from http://www.cal.org /caela/esl_resources/briefs/eslprogstandards.html

Rice, A. (Ed.). (2007). *Revitalizing an established program for adult learners*. Alexandria, VA: TESOL.

Roessingh, H., & Johnson, C. (2005). Online teaching and learning in TESL professional development. *The Quarterly Review of Distance Education, 6*(2), 107–115.

Russell, M., Coplan, R., Corrigan., C., & Diaz, R. (2003). *Factors influencing the effectiveness of a distance-learning model for professional development for teachers of adults: The case of ESL/Civicslink*. Philadelphia: National Center on Adult Literacy.

Sabatini, J. P., Daniels, M., Ginsberg, L., Limeul, K., & Russell, M. (2000). *Teacher perspectives on the adult education profession: National survey findings about an emerging profession*. Philadelphia: National Center on Adult Literacy.

Sabatini, J., Ginsburg, L., & Russell, M. (2002). Professionalization and certification for teachers in adult basic education. *Review of adult learning and literacy, 3*(chap. 6). Retrieved January 7, 2008, from www.ncsall.net/?id=572

Schaetzel, K., Peyton, J. K., & Burt, M. (2007). *Professional development for adult ESL practitioners: Building capacity*. Washington, DC: Center for Applied Linguistics. Retrieved January 7, 2008, from http://www.cal.org/caela/esl_resources/briefs/profdev.html

Shanahan, T., Meehan, M., & Mogge, S. (1994). *The professionalization of the teacher in adult literacy education*. Philadelphia: National Center on Adult Literacy.

Sherman, R., Tibbetts, J., Woodruff, D., & Weidler, D. (1999). *Instructor competencies and performance indicators for the improvement of adult education programs*. Washington, DC: Pelavin Research Institute. Available from www.eric.ed.gov

Sites, R. (1999, September). A user's guide to standards-based educational reform: From theory to practice. *Focus on Basics, 3C*(1), 3–7.

Smith, C., Hofer, J., Gillespie, M., Solomon, M., & Rowe, K. (2003). *How teachers change: A study of professional development in adult education* (Report No. 25a). Cambridge, MA: National Center for the Study of Adult Learning and Literacy.

Snow, M. A., & and Kamhi-Stein, L. (Eds.). (2006). *Developing a new course for adult learners*. Alexandria, VA: TESOL.

Teachers of English to Speakers of Other Languages, Inc. (TESOL). (2003). *Standards for adult education ESL Programs*. Alexandria, VA: Author.

U.S. Department of Education, Office of Vocational and Adult Education. (1992). *Model indicators of program quality for adult education programs*. Washington, DC: Author.

U.S. Department of Health and Human Services, Social Security Administration, & Office of Refugee Resettlement. (1995). *Mainstream English Language Training project (MELT) resource package*. Washington, DC: Author.

Van Duzer, C. H., & Berdan, R. (2000). Perspectives on assessment in adult ESOL instruction. *The Annual Review of Adult Learning and Literacy, 1*, 200–242.

Wrigley, H. S., & Guth, G. J. A. (1992). *Bringing literacy to life: Issues and options in adult ESL literacy* (ERIC No. ED348896). San Mateo, CA: Aguirre International.

Yogman, J., & Kaylani, C. T. (1996). ESP program design for mixed level students. *English for Specific Purposes, 15*(4), 311–324.

Glossary

action research: a process of reflective research and problem solving in which an individual teacher, a group, or a community of practice works together to improve their knowledge, strategies, and practices.

adjustment letter: a model response letter with specific sections: acknowledgment of the complaint, investigation of the complaint, outcomes of the investigation, resolution offer, and final apology and closure.

APPLE criteria: the NBPTS (National Board for Professional Teaching Standards, http://www.nbpts. org/, accessed 8/11/01) recommends that any assessment meet five criteria: administratively feasible, professionally acceptable, publicly credible, legally defensible, and economically affordable.

assessment-as-learning: part of a cycle of goal-setting and self-reflection where students and teachers evaluate their achievement of learning goals, considering what and how they learn. Helps students to develop metacognition.

behavioristic approaches: theoretical view that language learning is a matter of habit formation; learners mimic the language they hear, and when they receive some positive feedback, that language becomes a habit.

BEST test: Basic English Skills Test. There are two forms, BEST Literacy and BEST Plus, an oral proficiency test.

brainstorming: a writing heuristic and idea-generation strategy to help students develop ideas. Students list all ideas they can think of, writing them out either collectively or individually.

check-in: group members report to the class on the content and nature of their discussions (step 3 of Communication Seminar, or ComSem).

cloze activity: a method of language testing in which words are removed from a passage at regular intervals, and blanks are left in their place. Students must read the passage and try to fill in the blanks. Students may be scored based on either how many of the missing words they guessed exactly, or whether their guesses were appropriate and sensible given the context.

clustering: format for organizing students' ideas: the teacher writes students' ideas on the board as they volunteer them, grouping them by similarity; students then speak about anything that interests them from the cluster; often done as a pre-writing activity.

code switch: students switch to their own language, or from their own language into English; students may also switch between language varieties.

cognitive-affective filter: negative emotional and mental reactions that create a barrier between the listener and speaker and interfere with learning. Feelings like anxiety and self-doubt are examples of such emotions that can block learning.

Communication Seminar (ComSem): a project-based language learning approach with an emphasis on communication skills necessary for interaction in an academic community.

communicative competence: includes grammatical competence (syntactic, phonological, morphological, and lexical features of the language), discourse competence (ability to understand the relationship between words, phrases, and sentences as an interconnected and meaningful whole), sociocultural competence (understanding the social rules of language use), and strategic competence (coping strategies used in unfamiliar situations or when grammatical, sociocultural, or discourse knowledge is incomplete).

communicative skills: a language-teaching focus on using the language to communicate as opposed to only analyzing it; an artificial dichotomy that ignores the tremendous overlap between the two types of skills.

conditional: form of verb used with an if/then statement, for example, *If I had a million dollars, I would buy a mansion.*

conversation cards: card prepared by students or teachers in advance to use while engaging in a conversation. Students can create mind maps, draw pictures, or do anything that will serve as a memory aid while they are talking.

criterion references: measures of a student's mastery of the material; rather than measuring performance in relation to other students' scores or grades, criterion-referenced assessments measure individual students' performance in relation to the standard or learning goal.

dictocomp/dictogloss: a method for practicing composition in which the teacher reads a passage aloud and students write down what they understand and remember from the passage, staying as close to the original or original meaning as possible.

differentiated assessment: providing varied methods to assess student learning, in order to account for students' different needs, abilities, and learning styles.

discourse competence: the ability to interpret and understand longer sections of language as a whole; to use words, phrases, and sentences to put together coherent conversations and documents.

double-entry reading journal: a method for journal writing in which students divide the page into two columns. On the left, students copy a quote or summarize a passage from a text; on the right, they write their reactions and thoughts about the quote or summarized passage.

Downtown Landmark Project: a project at a private West Coast university in which students select a local landmark, learn about the landmark, survey locals, take photographs, and develop brochures about their landmarks to present to the class.

ear learners: students with strong English oral and social skills but with gaps in their academic preparation that affect reading, writing, and critical expression. These learners have usually been in an English-speaking environment/school for some time and have acquired their English through social interaction and talking. They are contrasted with **eye learners**, who have learned their English through reading (and writing), usually outside Englsh-speaking contexts.

English for academic purposes (EAP): branch of ESL/EFL that prepares students for academic work through English.

extensive reading: reading of English texts usually done by students on their own outside of the classroom.

F-1 visa: a full-time student visa for nonimmigrants wishing to pursue education in the United States.

four skill areas/four language skills: the four basic language skills are listening, speaking, reading, and writing.

freewrite, freewriting: students write for a set period of time, for example, 5 minutes, but do not get penalized for errors; provides an opportunity to use new vocabulary and to try out ideas on paper without frustration or fear of making mistakes.

Generation 1.5: students who have spent some time in the U.S. school system (usually at least secondary school) and have completed high school in the United States rather than in their native countries.

goal: specific statement about what students will achieve in a course or lesson. Goals define the purpose of a course or activity and drive lesson planning.

grammatical competence: knowledge of the syntactic, phonological, morphological, and lexical features of the language; the ability to correctly use the words, rules, and structures of a language.

indicators, teaching: descriptions of performances that show mastery of the standard.

information-gap activity: an activity in which each participant has part of the information and has to rely on the other participant(s) for the rest.

instructor-generated assessments: assessments designed by the individual instructor, not provided by a school system or prepared curriculum.

intensive reading: instructors explain the line-by-line meaning of texts, and translate if needed, with a focus on analyzing and understanding the structure and meaning of the text. May include identifying topic sentences, thesis statements, and cohesive devices, as well as practicing with new grammar and vocabulary. Based on these texts, the students complete grammar exercises to prepare for quizzes on vocabulary and structures.

jigsaw activity: an activity in which each participant is responsible for understanding and explaining a part of a text or assignment and sharing this information with a larger group of students; each participant provides a piece of the whole so that the group collectively gathers all necessary information. For example, divide the class into groups of four, each responsible for watching a different video segment while noting important information to share later with the others in their group so they can complete relevant postviewing questions on their handouts.

learning community: a group of people who share values or circumstances and who are engaged in education together and learn from each other. For example, combining a community of students who take an ESL reading class and a linked introductory psychology class.

lexicon: the vocabulary of the language.

life-skill competency approach: objectives for the course relate to life skills as does the standardized tests the students take at the beginning and the end of the term; these skills could include providing personal information, understanding transportation schedules, and giving information to a doctor.

literature circles: a type of book club in which the instructor acts as a facilitator rather than an authority, so students can have real-life discussions on readings. Each student in a small group plays either a general role (leader, recorder, reporter, or timekeeper) or a specialist role, such as identifying key vocabulary or memorable passages.

looping: a series of opportunities for students to reflect on the freewriting they have done, and write again using the previous ideas as starting points; each time students write by reflecting on their previous work, it is considered a new loop.

metacognitive awareness: awareness of one's own cognitive processes; the ability to reflect on one's own learning and thinking.

mind map, mind mapping: a method for recording ideas and discussion which is grouped into semantic categories; a graphic organizer.

morphology: a language's morphemic system, or the ways it combines and uses morphemes, the smallest meaningful units in a language (including prefixes, suffixes, and stand-alone base components). Also, the study of morphemes and their forms.

multitrait grading rubric: a rubric focusing on just a few specific dimensions of performance that are to be evaluated; these dimensions should be directly related to the purpose of the task. Such a rubric simplifies assessment and grading procedures and helps avoid excessive comments and questions that students may not be able to process.

muscle reading: a strategy for reading academic textbook passages in three phases: (1) preview, outline, and question; (2) read, underline, and answer; and (3) recite, review, and review again.

objective: knowledge and skills a teacher or student is expected to aquire by the end of instruction or a lesson.

oral interview: an interview that is designed to elicit language at progressively higher levels of proficiency.

outcome: specific, measurable description of what students should be able to understand or do by the end of the course or activity.

outcomes-based assessment: assessment designed to gauge students' achievement of intended outcomes; determining whether students have the specific skills and knowledge they were expected to gain.

paralinguistic clues: nonvocal elements like gestures and facial expressions that support and add meaning to verbal statements.

performance-based standards: standards that focus on demonstrable skills, knowledge, and dispositions rather than on content. Assessment of these standards is achieved using performance indicators.

performance indicators: statements that describe mastery of the standard; descriptions of ways a student can demonstrate that she or he has achieved the standard.

phonology: the study of the distinct sound units of a language, called phonemes; of the relationship between phonemes; and of the relationship between word combinations and sound patterns.

Plain English: a movement to create simple, straightforward language rather than academic, legal, or business jargon.

prepared participation: students are allowed thinking time prior to participation; helps everyone, but it allows the more reticent students to contribute.

schema building: activities which bring out relevant prior knowledge and understandings and relate them to a text or assignment.

situational English: language used in everyday situations.

skimming and scanning: two different reading strategies to quickly review material. Skimming involves reading certain sentences and sections, such as titles, subheadings, first sentence of each paragraph, or first and last paragraph of each chapter, in order to identify main ideas and arguments. Scanning involves searching for specific words or phrases, or specific informaton such as a name, date, or place.

SmallTalk: an activity in which students work in groups and discuss issues using social English: an opportunity for students to relax, enjoy themselves, and chat. In some activities, SmallTalk is followed by mind mapping, where students synthesize their discussions in order to do a third activity known as check-in.

sociocultural competence: understanding the social rules of language use and the ways that cultural context affects the meaning of what is said or written; being able to interact effectively in a particular social context.

sociolinguistic competence: the ability to understand and select appropriate uses of language for a given setting and audience. Language variety, word choice, and degree of formality should fit the circumstances.

standard: outline of what students or teachers need to know, understand, and be able to do; teacher standards provide guidelines to foster student success through effective teaching, allow prospective teachers and seasoned veterans to find opportunities for professional development and self-reflection, and provide teacher education programs and teacher trainers direction for their curricula. They can also be useful in establishing hiring criteria for evaluating candidates and assessing teacher performance.

standardized assessments: tests administered and scored in a consistent, uniform manner, and which have established norms.

strategic competence: ability to use coping strategies in unfamiliar situations or when grammatical, sociocultural, or discourse knowledge is incomplete; for example, avoiding grammatical structures that are not well-understood. To incorporate verbal and nonverbal strategies to compensate for difficulties in communication.

student-centered learning/student-centered teaching: an approach to teaching that focuses on the needs, skills, and interests of the students and encourages students to actively participate in their own learning; in this method, the teacher serves as a facilitator, rather than the sole authority in the classroom.

suprasegmental features (of English): features of the language such as pitch, volume, stress, and intonation, which stretch over more than one sound segment in a syllable, word, or phrase.

sustained-content approach: an approach used in both first and second language instruction in which one topic is used throughout a course; results in deeper levels of analysis, understanding, and vocabulary learning, as students read, think, and write about issues related to a single topic, rather than jumping from topic to topic.

syntax: the rules that govern how words may be combined to form sentences in a language; the study of how words are combined in sentences.

teacher-learner: teachers engaged in participatory, democratic, or student-centered teaching, in which the teacher co-participates in the journey of learning along with the students, serving as a guide but also learning from and with the students.

teacher talk: type and level of language employed by the teacher when addressing students.

textbook reconnaissance: reading strategy described in an ESL textbook, in which readers rapidly preview every page in a book, including the complete table of contents and appendixes.

transformational learning: a process of critiquing and questioning values, assumptions, and differing points of view; results in learning more than factual knowledge, instead changing one's worldview, attitudes, or actions.

yardstick: gradated descriptions of performances within a given skill area; used to measure student achievement and progress.